Are you serious about getting the most out of life and know the importance of your career in your life?

Do you know how your career affects your family, your well-being, your self-esteem, and your health and happiness?

Do you want to separate yourself from the pack, be more organized than anybody you have ever met, and more motivated and persistent than you ever thought you could be?

Do you need to protect yourself from economic and job market cycles, and the related governmental and regulatory dysfunction?

IF SO,

(1) You *MUST* have a disciplined **SYSTEM** for managing your career and protecting your life and family. *Making random calls and occasionally sending out a resume will not get you anyplace and will lead to frustration and disappointment.*

(2) You *MUST* learn how it identify career contacts and connections and to nurture and leverage these contacts to advance your career. *Don't limit yourself by relying on small networking groups and friends and associates from the past -- you need to reach beyond limited networking to identify your true scope of career contacts.*

(3) You *MUST* learn how to identify and evaluate career opportunities from events, announcements, publications, conferences, and online sources. *Randomly spotting career situations without an organized system will cause you to miss out on many real opportunities.*

"PREVAIL,EXCEL" will help you:
➤ Get your career organized
➤ Get serious about career opportunities
➤ Get your life and career back on track

 You need to get around all of the frustration, anger, discrimination and dysfunction in the career and job environment -- and start protecting your career, your family, and your life. That is the theme of this book: *Look out for yourself and your career, become directed and highly motivated and persistent, and adhere to a definite disciplined system.*

"*Prevail, Excel*" will help you survive and thrive in the chaotic job market, and will point you toward a lifetime of accomplishment and pride.

You are going to do this by:

(1) Becoming highly organized,

(2) Greatly increasing your level of motivation and persistence, and

(3) Setting up a complete *Career System* including a *Career Business Plan* and a *Career Marketing Plan,* and then *converting your plans to actions*, not just reading a lot of books and articles about jobs and careers, or occasionally sending out a resume.

"Prevail, Excel: Career Control Guide," can be ordered through Createspace.com/3738663 and Amazon.com. Go to the website *oportunitasmaximus.com* for more information.

i

PREVAIL, EXCEL:
CAREER CONTROL GUIDE

- ☐ How to Set Up a Disciplined Career System to Get Out of the Online Job Lottery and Protect Your Life

- ☐ Control Your Career In the Face of Economic Cycles, Mismanagement, and Political Dysfunction

- ☐ Develop and Nurture Your Career Contacts

- ☐ Identify and Leverage Career Opportunities

Fix Your Career Crisis

Opportunitas Maximus™

2012

ISBN-13:
978-1468020991

ISBN-10:
1468020994

First Edition

To my patient, supportive, intelligent, understanding, beautiful, and faithful wife, without whose guidance this effort would never have been completed.

This *Guide* is dedicated to the immeasurable power of the global information network, the Internet; and to those who remain aware of their potential in the face of global job market disarray, obfuscation and manipulation, and who insist on making their lives worthwhile every day.

****

CONTENTS

STEP 3 – MOVING AHEAD: YOUR CAREER ACTION PLAN

****

PREFACE

Today there is considerable confusion about job and career. When the economy is in a downturn, many are merely looking for any type of job, and jump at anything they can find. When the economy is in an upturn, job applicants have a choice among offers, and begin to think about what they really want to do, and think for at least a moment about the grandiose word *career* -- although they often fall prey to taking the job offer with the highest immediate salary, and only years later wonder what happened and what they could have done, and about career paths and choices.

But the current global economic disarray has imposed a new level of confusion on the career-and-job decision process. There is widespread job application discrimination and misrepresentation of the economy and the unemployment situation. And those trying to select a career path wonder if there is stability in any economic sector at all, given the confrontational environment surrounding governmental and regulatory policy.

As a unique individual in this world, you must protect yourself and your career and your life from the many undesirable elements in the economy. This *Guide* will help you do what the title says: *prevail* and *excel* in your career. It may take a while to develop a new level of discipline, motivation, and persistence, but it will be worth it. Going down the wrong path in your life could cost you a lot of money, and could cause you to be very unhappy. Don't blame yourself entirely if you have been diverted from the career that you had hoped for -- there are many distractions from a real career, and it has happened to many.

Prevail, Excel: is applicable to those in business, in government, and academia alike. The challenges and rules are the same across many sectors and segments of the global economy. As you will see,

vii

in all cases, there is a critical need for a *career plan,* a *career system,* and for a *deliberate action plan.* And your plan, systems, and actions must be constantly kept up to date. Without this disciplined structure, you will not succeed in controlling your life and your career.

Your career is not just one of the important things in your life -- it *is* your life. Some people will say that they go off to work just to have money to spend on things they like to do. Some people hate or resent the time spent on a job. Shame on them. The many hours, days, and years that slip away on their job represent a big piece of your life. You need to re-orient your life and do what you are good at and enjoy, and develop a feeling of accomplishment.

To build a career, you might have to change some fundamental things. Like learning to be extremely persistent and organized. And evaluating people who will help you and people who are not worth your time. And maintaining your skills and training. And upgrading your ability to speak and write. And learning to be positive and proactive, but never pushy-in-your-face. And remaining aware of changes within an organization and within multiple industry segments. And setting goals that will lead to accomplishments.

***

This *Guide* is divided into three parts, called *Steps.* **STEP 1: Where Are You, Who Are You?** gets you thinking in the right direction about job and career, and includes a discussion of the many angles and pitfalls in the job market and in managing your career. **STEP 2: How To Build a Career and Excel** delves into the many steps that you must take to define yourself and what you can do in this world and how you are going to go about it. The emphasis is on being extremely organized, and having a complete system for maintaining and developing your career. And **STEP 3: Moving Ahead: Your Career Action Plan** will help you get started immediately on a never-ending and winding path in life that will prove highly enjoyable. Each of these *Three Steps* has numerous *Sections.* You can skip around, but for many it will be best to follow the flow of the material as it is set forth, from 1 to 2 to 3.

This *Guide* is intended to be a practical working document. It has deliberately been kept short but to the point. No long extraneous prose about hypothetical careers or jobs. You can read many other books about such things, and the *Appendix* includes numerous resources that you might want to look over. But be careful - you can spend your whole life reading career books, sitting with career coaches, and listening to others. Eventually it will come down to who *you* want to be, and how to do what *you* want.

Enjoy *Prevail, Excel: Career Control Guide.* May we wish you the best of everything in the planning, control, and pursuit of your career.

𝕺𝖕𝖕𝖔𝖗𝖙𝖚𝖓𝖎𝖙𝖆𝖘𝕸𝖆𝖝𝖎𝖒𝖚𝖘™, 2012

****

1.1 SURVIVE & THRIVE IN YOUR CAREER

There is good reason for you to be outraged at the global job market disaster and the career confusion situation. There is open discrimination against the unemployed, the under-employed, and the mis-employed. When you hear monthly unemployment statistics on the news, these are merely "unemployment claims," namely those who have just filed for unemployment insurance. Although the cumulative unemployment total has declined in some segments, there are still a large number for whom unemployment insurance has run out and they still don't have a job, plus many who could contribute in the work force but have tried desperately and given up.

There is open age discrimination, and covert discrimination against women and many other groups. Many organizations are using temporary workers for many functions, so that they can dump them at will, and not pay any benefits. And many organizations are outsourcing a lot of jobs, to get people off the payroll and have the work done by someone at a lot less pay – but at much reduced quality and with customer frustration. Many companies are experiencing record profits, but they refuse to hire to meet demand, and instead are putting more money into automation in order to eliminate jobs, with officers paying themselves record bonuses. There is very little enforced regulation to correct the above situations.

You need to get around all of this discrimination and confusion -- and start looking out for yourself and your career and family, and protect your life from economic cycles and political dysfunction. That is the theme of this book: *Look out for yourself and your career, become directed and highly motivated and persistent, and*

adhere to a definite disciplined system. You must use your anger and frustration as a motivating factor to take control of your career.

"Prevail, Excel" will help you survive and thrive in the chaotic job market, and will point you toward a lifetime of accomplishment and pride.

You are going to do this by:

    (4) **B**ecoming highly organized,

    (5) **G**reatly increasing your level of motivation and persistence, and

    (6) **S**etting up a complete ***Career System*** including a ***Career Business Plan*** and a ***Career Marketing Plan,*** and then *converting your plans to actions*, not just reading a lot of books and articles about jobs and careers, or occasionally sending out a resume to a job posting to "see what happens."

This *Guide* is for those of you who are serious about getting the most out of life and who know the importance of their career in their life. The *Guide* is for those who have realized that they themselves must take responsibility for their career, that nobody else will do so. And it is for those who want to protect themselves from the many negative forces in the global environment which can derail a career and cause tremendous disappointment. Those who will appreciate the guidance of this book include the happily employed, the precariously-employed, the unemployed, and the many who are under-employed and mis-employed.

The title of this **STEP 1,** ***"Who Are You, Where Are You?"*** is not just an attention-getter, and these are not merely rhetorical questions. You need to be totally accurate about defining yourself and where you are in your life, in order to plan and shape your career. But we will get to this matter a little later.

2

Whether you are now employed in a very satisfying position or in a very shaky current position, or are between jobs, you need to manage your career. You must think *"career-not-job"* and make sure that you do not fall into the trap of thinking "job, any job" then *"career when I have time for it"* -- an approach that will assure that you will never get your life on track. You might bounce from job to job, chasing supposed "opportunities" as they seem to come along, and you could end up with a resume that is a mess, no in-depth skills, no satisfying sense of accomplishment, and damage to your own self esteem. Over your lifetime, this path could cost you a lot.

Your career is important. It must be coveted, protected, cultivated, and admired by yourself. Your career is not secondary to family, friends, and fun - it is *fundamental* to self-esteem, well-being, fun, and relations with family and friends. If you are not happy with your career, it will be impossible to be happy with how you assess your life. A successful career is paramount for a successful life, and a successful life must include a successful career.

One way of thinking about your career is that your are actually operating your own business over your lifetime. You are the principal investor, the CEO, and responsible for the return on investment. You must make careful decisions on all aspects and operations. You and only you are responsible for your career. *Cherish this responsibility* and do not expect to pass off or even share this responsibility with others, not your boss or any professional associates, or family or friends.

The job market today is in disarray, but you should not expect an orderly career opportunity and job situation, if it ever existed. There will always be economic and employment cycles over your lifetime, plus confusion factors related to mismanagement, governmental and regulatory dysfunction, and sometimes outright corruption. You need a career plan and system to make yourself "futureproof" in the face of such factors.

Much of the job posting and job search world has moved to the Internet, but beware -- many of the jobs posted on the Internet are old, and some never really existed and were scams – such as headhunter and human resources attempts to do "research" on available candidates and to find salary points. This is true for both company websites and the many popular job search sites. When an honest job is posted, so many electronic resumes and cover letters are sent and re-sent that it is impossible for human resources personnel or hired-third-parties to filter all but a sample, and often this filtering is done by dumb word-spotting software. So doing merely a straight-forward online job search can be unproductive and stressful -- you need to be much more clever in using online and many other resources. The sad side of online posting is that people feel that they are "doing something" that is useful in trying to apply online, but the probabilities are often so low that they in reality are just using up valuable time.

Stories abound about job candidates being selected purely at random, and well-qualified applicants being rejected out-of-hand and labeled as over-qualified by hiring managers and incompetent human resources personnel, who themselves sometimes are not qualified for their roles, and lack the self-esteem to select someone much more qualified, who would pose a threat to their own mediocre existence.

Company uncertainties and the accompanying bean-counter mentality often lead to a hiring freeze, but this is usually kept an internal secret while at the same time fake job openings continue to be posted - therefore needlessly wasting the time and raising the hopes of many applicants. Some companies dump highly experienced older employees who have many benefits, and at the same time hire younger inexperienced workers and pay them a lot less, with fewer or no benefits. Company pension plans are disappearing fast, often through a "freeze" via which new employees are locked out of having any pension, and even if they have a 401K, many companies don't even match employee contributions.

A resume-only approach is very demeaning – you put a lot of time into your resume and then you call to confirm receipt and some clerk can not even acknowledge that the job exists and hardly knows what is going on. You can end up sitting across a desk from some low level person who is screening candidates and can not even read correctly and has no idea what your background is all about much less the real requirements for the job. You are dressed up and ready to tell your story and what you can do for the company, and they merely want to get you out the door in ten minutes. Of course, if you are lucky to interview with the actual hiring manager, you can determine what kind of person you are dealing with, but often games are played with candidates, and the job and person that you thought you were applying for is not the actual reality. Sometimes they are very afraid of competitive analysis being conducted through job candidates, and will be guarded or even misrepresent actual company plans.

4

You need a much broader approach to job search and career development, and resume-submittal is only one element. In fact, a resume puts you in a very bad situation immediately. You become part of the crowd lining up for one or a few job openings that may actually be months away, or just part of somebody's future organizational planning and speculative budget.

An ***unsolicited proposal*** to the right person in a company often will have no competition at all, and you can start a dialogue that you can develop, nurture, and control. But more about identifying and working your own unique, secure, and qualified list of *career contacts* will be discussed later in this *Guide*. You will understand that to build such a list of contacts, you will need to establish and define yourself professionally, and have a highly organized process for identifying and communicating with others in your industry. This *Guide* will show you how to do this.

In addition to a warning about a resume-only approach, you should be aware that job-help information is voluminous, and spending hours and days on this can chew up a lot of your valuable time which you should budget carefully. There is information on the interviewing process, working with recruiters, dressing properly, how to take psychological tests, what to do about drug tests, negotiating salary, finding the hidden job market, dealing with a difficult boss, and on and on. You could spend your whole life just reading through this kind of stuff. Of course there are many elements in the job and career environment which deserve close attention. But this *Prevail, Excel: Career Control Guide* is focused much more on the real content, action plans, and substance of your career development.

This *Guide* will help you navigate, survive and thrive in the current chaos, and will point you toward a lifetime of accomplishment. You need a balanced program for your career and job search activities, and the *Prevail, Excel Guide* will tell you how to achieve this balance, and maintain it over your lifetime. Lastly, it will be emphasized that career planning and the pursuit of career opportunities requires a *very organized and structured system*, in order to be effective.

****

5

1.2 YOU AND YOUR CAREER

The first thing you must realize and affirm is that *you are the one in charge*. Nobody else is in charge. You may have experienced "control freak" managers who temporarily made you feel that you were not in charge. You may at times have seen yourself as a "victim" and have failed  to take responsibility for your own actions. And with the current job market chaos, you may feel that your own individual efforts are a minor factor in a bizarre situation. But rest assured -- who you are, and what you can contribute in this world is paramount. This is the reality, and not just "cheerleading."

Remember the quote: *"An optimist sees opportunity in every problem, and a pessimist sees problems in every opportunity"* -- Winston Churchill. It is your responsibility to maintain an optimistic outlook throughout your career, and to utilize your optimism to maintain control over your career.

You must think *career-not-job* -- whether you are currently employed in a very satisfying position or are between jobs. This might coom disloyal if you are a long-term valued employee, but you must always be prepared for changes which you do not control that might affect your livelihood and personal well-being. For example, at a small, closely-held company, the owners and investors can have a changing situation that prompts them to "take their money out" and sell off or even liquidate the firm. At a large company, there is always the possibility of a merger-acquisition, which can change things substantially. There is also constant pressure for companies to consider "outsourcing" or subcontracting functions which have traditionally been done in-house. Economic pressures from the now-mutilated financial institutions can further drive the mindless bean-counter mentality that has destroyed many firms. And then there are industry changes, driven by domestic or foreign competition, or because of the regulatory and legislative environment, including government equivocation, lobbying-driven reversals of once stable policies, and even outright corrupt actions.

So how do you remain in control of your career? *Answer:* By defining yourself and your goals and having a plan to achieve your goals -- not as a one-time activity, but on an ongoing basis, and this *Guide* will help you do this.

To help you in thinking about your career, consider the following quotations on the subject.

"If you wish to achieve worthwhile things in your personal and career life, you must become a worthwhile person in your own self-development." - Brian Tracy

"Your work is to discover your work and then with all your heart to give yourself to it." – Buddha

"The key to a happy and fulfilling future is knowing yourself. This self-knowledge is the most important component of finding the right career," – Richard Nelson Bolles, author of the acclaimed "What Color Is Your Parachute"

"I've missed more than 9000 shots in my career. I've lost almost 300 games. 26 times, I've been trusted to take the game winning shot and missed. I've failed over and over and over again in my life. And that is why I succeed." - Michael Jordan

"If people knew how hard I worked to get my mastery, it wouldn't seem so wonderful after all." - Michelangelo Buonarotti

"Work and Play are words used to describe the same thing under different circumstances." - Mark Twain

"No man can succeed in a line of endeavor which he does not like." - *Napoleon Hill*

"People don't choose their careers; they are engulfed by them".
                    – John Dos Passos

"The darkest day in a man's career is that wherein he fancies there is some easier way of getting a dollar than by squarely earning it." - *Horace Greeley*

"It doesn't matter who you are, where you come from.   The ability to triumph begins with you. Always. "   " I am seeking the fullest expression of myself as a human being on Earth." - Oprah Winfrey

"The supreme accomplishment is to blur the line between work and play." – Arnold Toynbee

"The privilege of a lifetime is being who you are"- Joseph Campbell

"Think not of yourself as the architect of your career but as the sculptor. Expect to have to do a lot of hard hammering and chiseling and scraping and polishing." - Bertie Forbes, founder of Forbes magazine

Lastly, a few warnings. There are many "career planning" websites, but a number of these are just trying to get personal profile information from you, either to market the data, or to give leads to career coaches, consultants, and even worse, predatory hackers and identity theft scammers.

Be careful what you provide, either on an opt-in website, a social networking site, through a blog, or a headhunter or job search site. Headhunters can sound very friendly and supportive, but anything you say could be recast and passed along to hiring managers and human resources departments, and is also subject to filtering and misinterpretation along the way. Also, if you post any information on Facebook, Linkedin, etc., make sure that it will help and not hurt you -- fellow-job-competitors can review and leverage anything put in the public domain. So, at this point, a couple of guidelines:

- *Blindly* trust no one, but be friendly, supportive, and helpful to all.

- Example: Your boss might be your "drinking buddy" but will fire you in a minute if told to do so or will lose his/her own job.

- Example: A well-qualified woman received a written job offer stating the day she was to start. She accepted the offer and showed up on the starting day, all dressed with her briefcase and ready to go. But as she got out of her car, the hiring manager came out to the parking lot and told her that there had been a "job freeze" and that the position was eliminated.

- Example: At a large aerospace company, one day they had a "fire drill" and all employees went out to the parking lot. Then some never-before-seen persons came out with bull-horns and read the names of those who should come back into the building, and that all others should go to their cars and leave the company, and that their personal belongings would be sent to their homes. This was the way they handled a mass-layoff.

- Example: An experienced technical worker received a job offer and then was flown out to the West Coast with his wife on a house-hunting trip. They found a house and put an offer on it and put their present house up for sale. Everything was packed to move to the new location. On the day they were ready to move, he received a call stating that the job had been eliminated.

****

1.3 YOUR SELF-IMAGE AND CAREER PERSONA

Now, back to the question posed in the title of this *STEP 1,* namely, *"Who Are You?"* It could also have been stated, *"Who do you want to be?"* For you to answer this question, you don't have to become overly introspective and engage in a self-psychoanalysis. But, you must be totally honest and objective. It is important to establish a clear and correct statement of your actual image, personality, and persona, so that you can fit your career plan with who you are and who you want to be. Here is a diagram of some of the many things that make us all unique and valuable in this world.

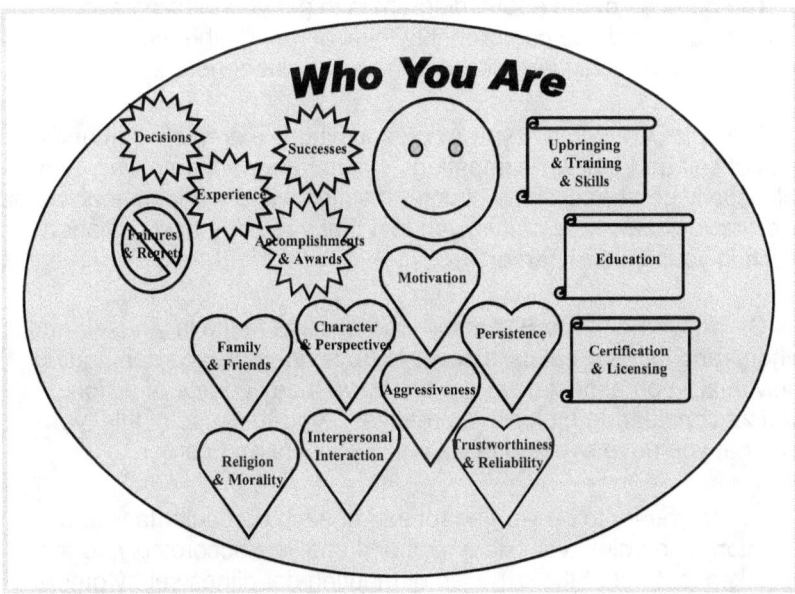

Those items in *hearts* are what are called the "affective" domain of ourselves, namely the core personality traits that we all exhibit. We are the product of our upbringing, including culture and religion, our developed character traits, trustworthiness, and reliability. We are shaped by our interpersonal interactions, especially by family and friends. And two important traits resulting are our level of motivation and persistence.

Those items in *stars* are what we have done or not done. We all have had many successes, both small and large. We all have made endless decisions, many good, some bad. And we also have received awards for our successes, even some rather intangible rewards to ourselves that have increased our own self-esteem.

And those items in *scrolls* are what we have learned. Even before starting school, we learned a lot of things from family, relatives, playmates, and friends. We all had various levels of formal education, but at the same time we continued to learn informally from our associates and surroundings, and the cultural environment. And work experiences up to the present also added to our lifetime learning.

The purpose of the above diagram is to get you thinking about who you are, and you can probably think of many other personal characteristics, achievements, and learning categories.

Example: Are you a "Type A" person who is extremely demanding, both of self and others, is impatient, would rather act than wait, and will usually go ahead with a course of action without a long analysis of alternatives. Because of this, you feel that you have accomplished much in your life and career.

Or, are you a "Type B" person who accepts faults in yourself and others, and takes great care never to be an in-your-face demanding individual. You almost never go ahead with any course of action without considering multiple alternatives. And because of this, you feel that you have avoided mistakes in your life and career.

Or, do you try to be very adaptable to each particular task and situation, and adjust your demands and analysis accordingly, to avoid mistakes, but not at the expense of meeting deadlines set by others and yourself. You feel that you try to avoid equivocation in setting priorities.

Do you like to plan everything, or do you enjoy "playing it by ear" since you feel that it is hard to predict things that you cannot control.

And so, you can see that it is not necessarily a simple task to assess exactly and correctly who you really are.

So here are a few things that you might do to assess yourself.

- First, write a short biography of who you are. Where were you born? Who were your parents and grandparents? How did you grow up? What was your earliest accomplishment that you now look back on? What were your early experiences and how did they shape your life? What were the major decision points in your life, and how did you make these decisions? Did you change course and why and how?

- When did you start thinking about what you wanted to do when you grew up, and how did you make that decision? Did anybody help you in the decision? Was it your own decision or were you coerced in any way?

- What was your education and training. How did you decide what to study in high school and in college or in any other training situation?

- List all of your likes and dislikes. List people you admire and people you detest.

- List your favorite entertainment. List hobbies and sports.

- If you are married or were previously married how did you make the decision on whom to marry?

- Describe yourself physically. Your health. Your looks. Your style of dress.

- List those you admire, role models, and why. And list those whom you think little of and why.

- Also list any and all opinions that others have expressed about you. Ask your spouse and friends about their opinion of you, in an indirect and well-phrased way. Think about both compliments and negative statements. Were the negatives coming from people who themselves were dysfunctional, or perhaps were jealous of you?

- Devise and ask yourself any other questions that you can think of yourself. Then document the answers to all of these self-assessment questions. But also document any open items that you cannot identify -- namely if you can't remember why you did something or details about something you think is important, then list these items for follow-up.

After you do this "self-assessment" then try to write down who you think you are. Namely, what kind of a person are you? What can you do, what do you know? How do you decide things? *Be very kind to yourself.* You probably know more than you first think, and can do many more things than you at first list. But begin to think about yourself in different situations. At work and at play. At home and away. In the presence of strangers and in the presence of loved ones and family and friends.

And lastly comes the hard part. How have you changed over time? How might you expect to change over your lifetime, namely what would you change yourself, and what might you be forced to change? If you were to change, how might you benefit from such a change? And regarding your very important career, what persona do you want to project?

Do not be afraid of adapting your persona to different activities in your life. You are not at all being a "phony" to act differently at work, at home, and at play; with professional peers in the workplace versus superiors; with customers; with friends and family; and with adults versus children. But regarding your career persona, you must be consistent and appropriate to the applicable context and culture.

If you need further background on defining your career persona, go to the *"Persona"* section of the *Appendix*, for a number or related references that will help you.

****

1.4 CONSIDER WHERE YOU ARE NOW

In addition to the above self-assessment to answer the question *"Who are you,"* you need to assess where you are in your life and career at this moment in time, namely *"Where Are You Now?* For example, you could be:

- Between jobs
- Underemployed in whatever you are doing now
- Going back for additional education or training
- Retired but desiring to go back to work
- Happily employed but keenly aware of instabilities in your current situation
- Employed but dissatisfied, or experiencing conflicts
- Employed but desiring to change your career focus
- Happily running your own business but aware of market instabilities
- Running your own business but experiencing many difficulties

And so forth. Try to define your current situation precisely and in detail. Write down what you think and look it over again and again. Be fair to yourself but scrupulously honest.

If you are angry about unemployment, an unfair job situation, or poor employee treatment, you must come to terms with this anger and learn to *convert it to motivation and action,* so that it does not derail your career management and control. We will discuss more on this matter later in the book.

Now some examples.

- You could be very satisfied in a current job, but so focused on the work and people around you that all you think of is one company. You might not be paying enough attention to what is happening in your industry and with competitors. You also might not know much about the financial condition of your company, including what financial analysts and investors think. If this is true, you could be in danger, since your satisfying situation could change drastically and rapidly.

- You could be employed in a rewarding position, but too focused on the immediate job market, always checking online job listings (many of which are not real jobs), to the exclusion of managing your current situation and personal career development.

- You could be a person (like many), who went to school and feel that you are done with that for the rest of your life. You have kept away from any educational programs, training, self-education, and certification. Any learning has been company-focused OJT (on-the-job training). If this is true, you could be way out of date in your field, greatly reducing your value in the career marketplace.

- You could be licensed in a particular trade or hold a particular certification and have a lot of experience, but are assuming a passive role in job assignments, waiting for the phone to ring with a request from customers, general contractors, or contract agencies. When business cycles occur, you hunker-down and wait for a recovery. You stick to one trade, skill, or certification and wait it out.

- You could be unemployed for a long time, having sent out thousands of resumes, had interviews, and received a few job offers for very undesirable situations at pay far below what you have gotten in the past. You are not sure what to do now.

- You could be intensively "networking" to find a job. You go to networking groups almost every day, and tell your story, and listen to others say how they used to manage hundreds of people, but one day their job was eliminated, and at their age nobody wants them. You spend a lot of time chasing even the lowest probability job opportunity that you hear about. It takes you almost a whole day to do a cover letter, adapt a resume, make related phone calls to confirm receipt. Often you spend $20 to send a resume via overnight carrier to get your response to a newspaper ad in immediately.

Now, to add some structure to your assessment of *"Where You Are Now,"* you need to break down the assessment into a number of categories, The best way to help yourself is to make a chart, like the example shown below. Look at this as a worksheet or template to guide the self-assessment of where you are now. You might want to add your own elements to the Assessment column. The point is that you need to organize and document your assessment.

18

Assessment Category	Past	Present	Future
Employment or unemployment situation			
Self-employment or ventures (if applicable)			
Financial situation and outlook			
Skills *(all the things that you can capably do)*			
Education *(formal, including both degree and non-degree programs)*			
Training *(shorter term)*			
Self-Learning			
Certification			
Licensing			
OJT			
Seminars, webinars			
Conferences			
Internal Publications			
External Publications			
Internal Presentations			
External Presentations			
Experience *(jobs held, things accomplished)*			
Difficulties Overcome			
Opportunities Missed			
Good Decisions			

Bad Decisions			
Successes *(both your own initiatives and things that just happened)*			
Failures *(things tried which did not work out)*			
Personality traits			
Perspectives			
Hobbies			
Etc.			

The above table is merely an *example* of your own continuing assessment of the "here-and-now" of your life and career. A table for your own individual self-assessment is a personal task for you to undertake. Do not see it as a one-time exercise that you put in a drawer and forget about. This is your own honest report card of *"where are you?"* But you need to maintain a complete and ongoing assessment of where you are and where you are going.

This ends *Section 1.4* on *"Where You Are Now"* in your career. The next section is going to address the overall matter of career planning.

****

1.5 CAREER PLANNING BASICS

Step back for a moment and consider what career planning is all about. It is not a simple matter of "defining yourself" first, then "making career choices." It is certainly not "you against the world" nor is it "you accommodating to the world." It is more like "you and the world working together." There are a few things that you can change, and many things that you cannot change, but with the proper career, there is much that you can accomplish in your lifetime.

So understanding the realities and dynamic conditions of the real world is basic to your career planning. This is true whether you choose to spend most of your life in the academic, religious, industrial, profit-directed, non-profit, or volunteer environment. Do not think that career planning is all introspective and practically  requires a psychoanalysis of your motivations and desires. You must orchestrate many elements regarding your capabilities and opportunities, and develop a very deliberate and persistent focus, and constantly review and update your planning.

And you do not have to be "one dimensional" in your thinking. You can plan for multi-career paths over your lifetime. A plan like working in one or more industries, followed then by teaching or focusing on helping others and volunteering. Or traveling the world to learn what is really out there, then finding your own career niche and settling in one location and one industry, or deliberately working in a series of environments in several selected locations.

Your plan might be "to play it by ear" and have a broad enough education, retraining-as-needed, and perspective to take advantage of opportunities that will arise and are hard to define specifically ahead of time. Or your plan might be to learn a particular profession and specialty in depth, and to stick to this throughout your life as far as possible.

The idea of having a dynamic and living career plan is basic. Without a plan, it will be difficult for you to maintain control of your life. Obviously, no matter how directed your career goals and objectives, many events can and will occur over your lifetime which require contingency career planning, and "rainy day" scenario planning. You do not want to be naïve to think that you can control everything in your life, but you need to make sure that unplanned changes do not derail your career plans and drive you to a state of paralysis.

As you well know, some people devote themselves to one company in a very loyal and dedicated manner, accomplishing many things. Then they wake up one day and are told that the company has been acquired and their job is being eliminated. Or the company sinks into economic difficulty and a force-reduction is imposed and they are told to leave. Or the dedicated employee stays in one position for their whole life, watching others pass them by, wondering why they are still stuck in the same job. Those who never plan can be thrown into a depressed state, from which they never really recover for the rest of their life. You do not want to be one of these.

A living career plan and orchestration of all the elements that support and go into the plan will be a positive motivating factor for your life. You will wake up every day with objectives and goals in mind, knowing that you have a plan and direction in your life. Your self-esteem and optimism will radiate and touch everyone and every situation that you face.

To help you in your thinking, the following is a table of the four fundamental sectors of the global economy. Within these four there are many sub-segments of the economy, and of course thousands of career choices and opportunities.

Sector	Examples
Primary Extraction	*Mining, petroleum and natural gas drilling, agriculture, fishing, energy extraction, ...*
Manufacturing	*Automotive, aircraft, military, electronics, computer, food manufacturing, ...*
Services	*Medical, retail, education, financial, religion, police, fire, security, ...*
Information	*Entertainment, publishing, TV, arts, culture, R&D, ...*

The global annual economy is over 70 trillion dollars, and the U.S. annual economy is over 15 trillion dollars. Globally, there are about 2.75 billion people employed, and 139 million employed in the U.S. in civilian jobs. The main point here is that the global economy, in good

22

times and bad, is a multi-trillion dollar environment, with billions of people involved in a vast array of careers, and new opportunities arising daily. It is up to you to build your path in this environment, and this *Guide* will help you formulate your plans for doing so.

Many bemoan the current condition of the world's economy and the situation in the U.S. and Europe in particular. But look at the realities. The world is in transition between the old industrial developed countries and many other developing countries, and this transition is the norm and will not go away. Some industries remain important and are almost "futureproof." Like the global demand for energy. Like health and nutrition and well being. Like education. But all industries have cycles and local pockets of problems and issues to be recognized, managed, or avoided. Growth areas continue: nursing and medical assistants, communications networking, the Internet, software, and on and on. Some of these areas are vulnerable to outsourcing and offshoring – like routine web design, routine computer programming, human resources record-keeping, routine accounting, routine legal research, routine medical image reading, etc. And some things will never be outsourced offshore – like fixing a car, cooking and restaurant services, installing and servicing entertainment and communications systems, live performing arts, and many others. Some areas are cyclical, like construction, housing, and defense spending. So segments of the economy must be closely monitored as you plan and progress in your career.

If you want to dig further into the various economic sectors, career categories and job statistics, please go to the *Appendix*, and you will find many online links that will help. Although these data may be interesting, the data itself will never tell you what you want to do in your life or how to manage your career. Rather, emphasize for yourself the positive aspects of your life, what unique skills you have or can develop further, and how these unique skills will lead you to success and happiness. In looking at any links and references, first prepare yourself to be very directed, goal oriented, and time-management-focused in utilizing these resources.

Another basic way to look at career paths is to think about those careers that span many economic sectors and also those careers that are limited to a particular sector. For example, sales is applicable to virtually all of the above sectors, and could be called a "horizontal career path" since sales training and experience can be applicable across sectors. Of course, many actual job requirements can state that sales experience is needed in a particular field, but someone who

23

has successfully sold manufactured goods might also be well qualified to sell services also, especially within the same industrial sector where they might already have a number of contacts. Another horizontal career path is computer and IT (information technology) services. Just about every sector needs an Internet presence, and most sectors are also dependent upon communications technology. On the other hand, some career paths are focused only on one particular economic sector and a narrow segment. A fisherman or a farmer might have difficulty moving to certain other segments, but with the proper training and perspective, many people certainly have been successful in changing career orientation. In fact, someone who has grown up on a family farm or has worked on a family fishing boat, might have a career plan to stay in the family business for a period of time, and then transition to a particular profession after they complete the required training or certification.

There are many stages in one's lifetime, from infancy to maturity, but for our purposes here, we have defined *Ten Career Stages*, as depicted in the following.

	CAREER STAGES	
1	Childhood initial development, fantasies, guidance and exposure; ages 3 – 7	10 years
2	Child investigating life choices with guidance and exposure, early experiences; ages 7 – 10	
3	Young adult learning and preparing for career decisions with guidance and active experiential participation and counseling and making educational choices; early career roadmap; ages 11-18	15 years
4	Young adult attending college or other training, starting work, continued guidance, initial experiences, proactive role, gathering information, initial career roadmap developed, ages 18-25	
5	Young adult starting career, managing career, starting lifelong learning, updating and following career roadmap, ages 26-35	45 years
6	Young adult approaching middle age, managing career, continued lifelong learning, updating and following career roadmap, ages 35-50	
7	Middle age, managing career, continued lifelong learning, updating and following career roadmap, ages 50-60	

8	Older active adult, managing career, continued lifelong learning, updating and following career roadmap, ages 60-70	
9	Mature adult, career options and lifelong learning options, ages 70-85	15+ years
10	Elderly adult, age 85+	

Probably the most important aspect of these *Career Stages* is *preparation*, namely both individually and with guidance, preparing for future events and career decisions. Even between early childhood and up to about age 10, there should be guidance and exposure to "what people do in life." Sometimes fathers and mothers will bring young children to their own work location, and sometimes tours are arranged through schools and other organizations of particular buildings, industrial, locations, governmental locations etc. to help guide children. Between the ages of 11 and 18, adolescents and teenagers need to seriously develop career choices, including skills needed, educational requirements, and should draft a first career roadmap. They should be given a lot of support in this, but should be nurtured to gradually develop their own decision-making skills, including gathering information, talking to people, joining groups, and taking on a responsibility for their own lives and careers. Sometimes formal education and career preparation will continue until the age of 25 or beyond for specialty training, and sometimes young adults will start working in their teens. For some persons, the best preparation for life is a work-study program in which they immediately experience the real world and continue their formal education at the same time. And for others, the best preparation for life is to have work and travel experiences prior to then devoting themselves to formal education. It can be a shock for some persons who were "shielded" from the real world, and then start working for the first time after many years of formal education and camp, play, and travel. At that point they might not adapt very well and might not make decisions on their own properly. Improper decisions at an early age are forgivable and recoverable, but at an older age such mistakes can be devastating and costly.

The longest career cycle period on the chart above is the approximately 45 years that an adult is directly involved in pursuing their career development. This is the primary focus of this *Career, Excel – Career Control Guide,* and during this career phase, the *CareerRoadmap* is a principal living document for staying on track and executing mid-course-corrections . Some people are capable of and desire to work in various capacities to age 70 and beyond. In our opinion, the worst life plan is for a person to want to "retire" as young as possible and have no plan at all. Today, some persons are fortunate enough to build up financial security at a relatively early age, but then leverage this financial security into career activities that they themselves find rewarding, including ventures and volunteer activities.

The last career cycle period depicted above is the mature years of age 70 and beyond. Although many people are not working at all during this period, some people are definitely very active in their careers. For example, they might then be a very valuable partner and asset in a particular professional services firm, like a medical or law practice, but be able to control their own level of involvement in activities of that practice, depending on a balance with their own personal interests at that point in life. They might also have built up a business themselves, and be very involved in turning over the business to a younger generation.

In summation, the subject of career life cycles is an important way of thinking about career choices that fit with where you are in your life. If you are involved in helping others with early career decisions, including children, adolescents, and young adults, then understanding career stages is very important.

Before we go to the next section, which focuses on laying out your career specifics, you need to assess where you are now in terms of understanding career planning basics. Only *you* can do this assessment. If you think that you need to educate yourself further on career planning, then look at the reference items in the *Appendix* as a guide. But do not let yourself get overly absorbed in these basics to the exclusion of practical career planning -- that is the focus of this *Guide*. Here are some points to consider in assessing your knowledge and understanding of the basics of career planning.

- You cannot decide *exactly* what you want to do for all the rest of your life, since there will be many changes that you cannot control that will occur throughout your life. Be prepared for changes in the environment, and changes in yourself. Be prepared to adapt to the environment, and to pursue education, training and updating accordingly.

- Deciding your "mission in life" is not an easy one-time exercise, but rather a decision that you will make and then modify as needed. It is OK to be lofty about your mission, but then follow up by getting your feet on the ground and keeping them there.

- So making the correct decisions at any particular time in your life is an important skill that you must develop, nurture, and strengthen. What is you own personal process for making the correct decision? Can you improve your personal decision-making process?

- Career counselors can help, but they cannot and should not choose a career for you – that remains your own personal decision. Sometimes people take "aptitude tests" that supposedly tell them what they are good at and what they are not good at. But remember, success depends primarily on your own motivation and persistence, not what comes out of a test that somebody designed with an idea of how to choose careers.

- Deciding what you want to do in life is not a decision made in a vacuum, and is best made after you saturate yourself with real information, obtained from a wide variety of reference information and personal interactions.

- If you are not sure what goes on in a particular field, contact the applicable trade group or association or governmental or academic or religious or nonprofit or volunteer organization and gather information, and follow up on any personal contacts and face-to-face discussions that they can facilitate.

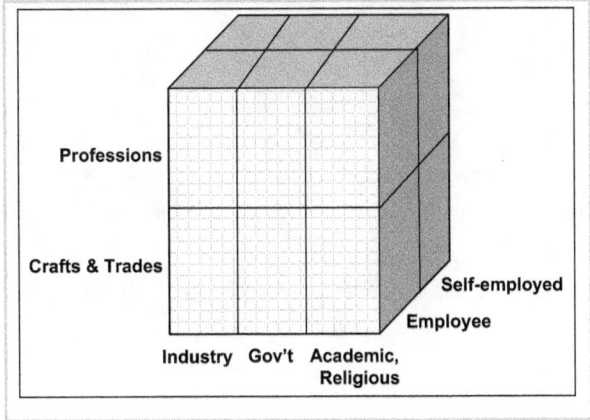

- Make sure that you expand your thinking beyond a narrow professional or trade category. Look at the diagram above, and remember that many segments of activity are open to you.

- *The bottom line – it is up to you.* Career choice is a personal responsibility and individual right. Relatives and friends and associates might tell you what they think you should do, but we are past the time when some dictator or royalty figure could decide your life for you. Cherish this responsibility.

****

1.6 TAKE IT A STEP-AT-A-TIME: BUILD YOUR CAREER ROADMAP

There is a lot for you to do to get your career or job search on track. But you must not be overwhelmed. You need a *plan*, and a *CareerRoadmap*, the various elements of which are depicted in the diagram shown here, should be the primary tool for developing and updating your *Career Plan*. A *CareerRoadmap* consists of an orchestrated mix of elements, planned together and coordinated, to help you deal with choices, environmental factors, and decision paths. There is no perfection here, but such a *Roadmap* will be a big help in organizing your career. A diagram of your *Career Roadmap* is shown below.

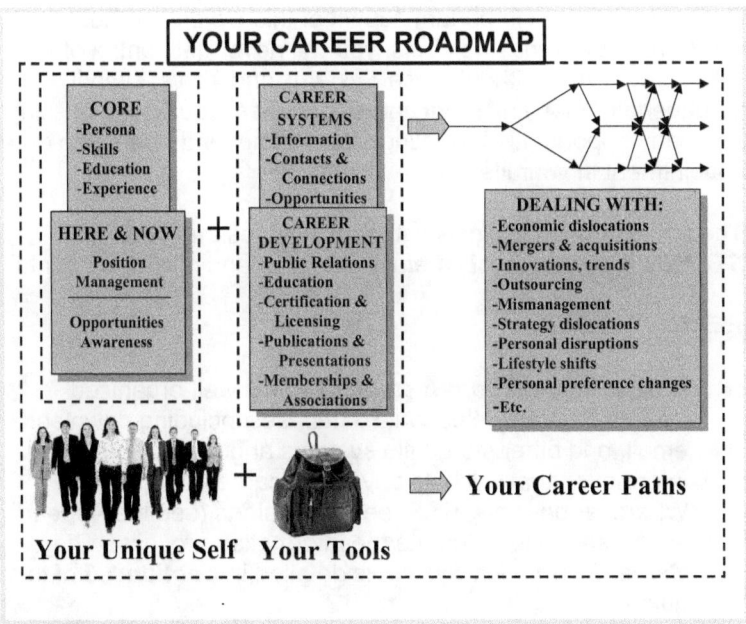

The first dotted box of your *CareerRoadmap* is designated *"Your Unique Self."* In the **CORE** area of this dotted box are *four elements* defining yourself: Your **Persona** (who you are and your perspectives), your **Skills** (what you are capable of doing), your **Education** (formal training and-or certification), and your **Experience** (what you have accomplished and jobs held).

The second group in the *first dotted box* of your *CareerRoadmap is designated* **HERE & NOW**, *and* includes the following:

HERE & NOW

- ***Position Management:*** What you must do to optimize your career opportunities in your current career position. This is detailed in **Section 2.1** of this guide.

- ***Opportunities Awareness:*** What you must do in your current career position to remain aware of opportunities within your company, and also what you must do to remain aware of opportunities within the industry. This is detailed in **Section 2.5** of this guide.

Moving to the right in the *Your CareerRoadmap* diagram includes a number of ***"Tools"*** that will get you in control of your career. These are probably the most important aspect of this *Guide*. Without the proper *Career Systems* and *Tools*, you will never get control of your life and career. And without these *Systems* and *Tools*, even if you might undertake many different career activities, you will be missing out on many opportunities, wasting a lot of time, and headed to great disappointment in your life.

The first group in the *Tools* category includes the **CAREER SYSTEMS** which you must carefully establish and diligently maintain:

CAREER SYSTEMS

- ***Career Information System:*** This is a well-organized system, primarily electronic databases including downloads, email, and other stored file systems and databases, for all information that will help drive your career planning. Wherever possible, RSS feeds and alerts (see the *Appendix*) will be set up to automate the information process. The *Career Information System* is detailed in **Section 2.3** of this guide.

- ***Career Contacts and Connections System:*** A process for identifying, screening, and maintaining listings of persons who can help you with career opportunities, plus the process of nurturing and interacting with these persons. This *System* is detailed in **Section 2.4** of this *Guide*.

- ***Career Opportunities System:*** The *Career Opportunities System* is detailed in **Section 2.5** of this guide.

The second area of *Tools* for successfully controlling your career is labeled **CAREER DEVELOPMENT** and includes the following:

CAREER DEVELOPMENT

- **Career Marketing and Public Relations:** This is the important process of telling the world who you are, what you can do and have done, and making sure that your persona and identity are protected and aligned with your career goals. This is detailed in **Section 2.6** of this *Guide*.

- **Career Education Program:** The process of adding to your original formal education, via degree-focused and non-degree programs, both live and online, with various supporting media, in order to advance both your personal development and your career opportunities. This is detailed in **Section 2.15** of this guide.

- **Career Certification and Licensing Program:** The process of obtaining verification of your expertise level in a particular discipline and field, generally through third-party organizations that conduct testing, for the purpose of personal development and advancement of career opportunities. Detailed in **Section 2.14** of this *Guide*.

- **Career Publications and Presentations:** The process of documenting, both publicly and privately, through an appropriate media mix, your ideas, innovations, accomplishments, perspectives, and reactions to the environment and the works of others. Also, the process of delivering, verbally with supporting media, your ideas, perspectives, solutions, and related information, both privately and publicly, to appropriate audiences. These are detailed in **Section 2.11** and **Section 2.13** of this guide.

- **Career Memberships and Associations:** Personal association with trade groups, advocacy groups, and other professional associations which have been established to advance knowledge and public awareness and support in a particular field, and to aid the professional development of members.

YOUR CAREER PATHS

The third major area of importance in the *CareerRoadmap* above concerns your **Career Paths.** Listed in the diagram are a number of events and factors which can affect the paths that your career will take over your lifetime, and the pictorial diagram with arrows merely is to indicate that you yourself can redirect your career and also should be prepared for changes over your lifetime. The list is endless, but should include both your planned career path and unplanned career path items. The primary importance of your *CareerRoadmap* is to develop and use the *Tools* described here to control your own career paths, and not be merely driven helplessly by events and circumstances. *Section 1.5 Career Planning Basics* discussed laying out your career options, and *Section 2.2 Developing Your Career Business Plan* will discuss the matter of forecasting your career options and earnings.

Planned Career Path Changes

Of prime importance in your life are the things which you yourself initiate and control, as opposed to things to which you must react wisely on a contingency basis. Continuously throughout your life you should review where you are and who you want to be and where you want to be. *Never* just let things happen or stay in a position to "see what happens."

So, first, your *planned career path changes* should include these elements:

1. Every 3-4 years, you should establish a **Short-Term Career Phase Gate**. This will be a decision point to assess where you are and where you want to be, and what steps should be taken at this point.

2. At these *Phase Gates*, you should establish **Career Decision Criteria**. For example, you might establish that if you are not promoted or achieve the compensation you desire, then you will change positions, either within the organization or move externally. Or if you have not expanded your capabilities and value in the marketplace to the extent you desire, because of limitations in your current position, that you might need to make a change. Or you might have decision criteria related to keeping up with the industry and developing career contacts, and that your

current position is limiting your ability to do so, because of the routine and repetitive and scheduling nature of the particular current position. Or if you are totally satisfied with your progress at a *Career Phase Gate*, then your decision might be to stay in the current position for another 2 years and monitor things carefully. For planned career path changes, these career decision criteria will be under your control, as opposed to things not under your control to which you must react.

3. Remember that you must be totally accurate and honest in planning, assessing, and developing your career. If your *Career Decision Criteria* at a *Career Decision Point* have not been met, ask yourself if you have done all that you planned to meet these criteria. Namely, if you were aiming for a promotion and did not achieve this, did you do everything in terms of accomplishments, nurturing of contacts, developing of capabilities, career marketing and public relations, that you needed to do. If the answer is yes, then consider a change. If the answer is no, then will a change spur you to increase your motivation and persistence in order to meet your criteria.

4. You must also establish **Long-Term Career Phase Gates**. For example, you might have a goal to establish your own business at some point in your life, after having worked for one or more companies to learn all the details of an industry. Or you might have a goal of starting your own business immediately after completing your career training, but then either selling off the business at some point, or transitioning the business to your children or business partners. You might have a goal of working overseas, after first working domestically for a multinational company. Or, you might have a goal of working in an industry, and then transitioning to a teaching or religious or non-profit or volunteer situation. For any *Long-Term Career Phase Gate*, you should try to put a date on the event, and think of steps that will lead you to this change.

5. At a *Career Phase Gate*, you must also totally review your *Career Business Plan*, and all the elements of your *Career Roadmap*, namely your education, accomplishments, skills, contact inventory, career opportunities base, publications and presentations, certifications, and association memberships. If you do not like what you see, then you must make changes.

33

Unplanned Career Path Changes

We do not control everything in this world, but we *can* control how we react to unplanned changes, and in fact how we react to such unplanned changes defines who we really are. Often, until people are tested by changes and adversity, we do not really know their character and true persona. As you go through this *Guide*, you will see much material about developing your career contacts, building your capabilities and marketability and career public relations, and also developing contingency plans. But at this point, regarding development of your *CareerRoadmap*, remember that the total mix of planned and unplanned career path changes will constitute your career throughout your lifetime. *(Later on in the Sections of Step 2 of this Guide, you will find a full discussion of the steps which you must take to protect yourself from unplanned career path changes, and to make yourself very robust and virtually futureproof as far as your career is concerned.)*

Suggestions for Formulating Your Career Roadmap

Taken together, the elements of the above diagram constitute your *CareerRoadmap*, all integrated in an holistic manner, and orchestrated to achieve the best career path for yourself. Now, here are some additional suggestions on formulating the *Roadmap*.

- **Assess Your Skills, Experience: Past, Present, and Future**

  Ask yourself the following questions. What can you do? What have you done? Did you ever publish anything? If yes, build a record of copies. Have you given talks – if so, likewise build a record of all of these, both internally and in public. What do you like and dislike? What do you hate? What would make you stay up all night? Where do you want to be? If you didn't have to work, what would you do that would lead to your most important lifetime accomplishments?

  In answering these and similar questions that you should ask yourself, do not overlook even the most minute details. Sometimes something small in your background and experience can make a big difference and become the springboard for a new career direction.

  In assessing your skills and experience, you need to look at the past and the present, and then set goals for the future. What skills do you lack that you want to add, and when, and how? What skills need improvement and updating and how will you do this and when?

* **Inventory and Assess your Education, Training, Certification**
Go back in your thinking to high school – what did you focus on, what were you good at, then the same for college and any other training that you have had. Get your records in order, and call or email to get copies of anything that you need. Make copies of degrees, certificates, class completion documents. Be critical of yourself. Is any of this training still applicable to the real world today? Do you need to bring yourself up-to-date? Did you hate what you studied, and wish that you studied something else? What possible additional training do you need now? Did you receive informal training from anybody at all ? -- via a family member, neighbor, or friend on anything, such as computer programming, house painting, electrical work, plumbing, automotive repair, sports training, sales, medical knowledge, financial insights, etc. And include anything else in your experiences – languages, techie topics, human relations, voluntary experiences.

Set goals and objectives in the categories of *Education, Training,* and *Certification* but be careful to not get carried away. Be realistic and establish timeframes and specify how you will achieve these goals.

* **Create an Ongoing List of Contacts**
Start with those with whom you have been associated in the past that you might keep in touch with in support of your career. If you are now working, include management figures, co-workers, and associates. Get their email addresses, physical addresses, and telephone numbers. Then list what they can do to help you. Discard any names that might be trouble or cannot help you. We're talking about your career -- don't start including friends just for the sake of it.

The whole idea of "job networking" is really overworked. You don't want to start leaning on friends to sneak you into a job where you don't fit or cannot contribute anything. A local "job network" is often very limited to the narrow scope and perspectives of the group members, maybe a dozen or so people - where they happened to have worked, who they know, who are their friends and neighbors, what is the latest rumor or hearsay. *This is not a very solid foundation on which you can build a career.* At best, you are likely to merely bounce from one job to another depending on the vagaries of a local job networking group. You also don't want to "network" with a group of unemployed persons who keep asking each other "what have you heard?" "Did you apply for this or that job?" "Did you see that new job ad in the newspaper?" "When did you get laid off?" Their negative stories will be a de-motivator for your career outlook and esteem-building.

Don't waste your valuable time on often non-productive and low-probability hearsay activities. On the other hand, if you are lucky enough to hear of a "perfect fit" where you can contribute because of your own unique background and experience, do not hesitate to follow up *immediately* to find out if this is a true career opportunity, and be prepared to tell them what you can do for the company. *We will discuss more about building a great contact list later in Section 2.4 of this Guide.*

- **Build An Inventory of Opportunities**
Think positive and think "opportunities," not "problems." *(As mentioned before, Winston Churchill once said: "Pessimists see a problem in every opportunity, and optimists see opportunities in every problem.")* Go online and subscribe and opt-in to every publication and trade item that you think might help you find opportunities -- if you overdo it, you can cancel out. Look for articles that could help your career and job situation, take down names and titles, and any related helpful information. The *Appendix* lists many resources and publications that will help in this scanning for opportunities. Here are some guidelines for such scanning:

    ✓ Develop a *system and process* for going through a publication, online article or blog or review. Do not just read through the whole item for entertainment. Your focus is to look for opportunities.

    ✓ Look for both names and topics of relevance. Even if the item is not well written or of little consequence itself, you might see a well-positioned name in a company or field that is of interest to you. Officer levels or a person in charge of something hot should be given priority.

    ✓ Immediately associate in your mind how you would follow up on the item found. That is, think of a letter or email congratulating them on their publication and particularly commenting on the things that they have said, and relating what they have said to opportunities in the industry, and your own perspectives. In other words, "handles" for a follow-up. Your goal at this point is merely to think of how you might elicit a response from the author of the item, to "test them out" to see if they are "closed" or "open" in their persona and perspective. *Do not ever at this point think of asking them for a job.* You can tactfully mention something in your own background of relevance, and your own perspective. But be careful about throwing your opinions around when you don't really know this person at all.

✓ Even advertisements can tell you something about a company and possible opportunities. In some publications, you can order a follow-up be sent to you with more information about a particular product or service. If a company is advertising for people in a print ad, the opportunity for you might be to mention that they will need managers to direct the efforts of staff additions.

✓ It is useful to be timely in a response to a published item found, but sometimes a later follow-up can be of relevance if there happens to be another event in the industry -- things like regulatory changes, competitive announcements, technical breakthroughs, etc.

Do the same as the above for trade shows and events. Go to related blogs. Go to company websites and do the same. Get annual reports. Build new directories on your computer. Buy a memory stick or a stack of DVDs or CD-ROMs and store this new information in an organized manner, maybe even a formal database. Download documents of interest. Then create and index and organize a list of opportunities that are of relevance. If you think that you might want to change fields, and are capable of such a change, then broaden your horizons. For example, the emphasis on energy markets and energy innovations will not go away, but might be too big a change for you to take on if you don't have the background and flexibility. But if you are a sales person with great sales experience and flexibility and skills, and think that you can contribute in many fields, don't flinch at looking at new market segment opportunities.

- ***Build An Opportunities Follow-Up List and Plan***

Now we're getting to where the rubber-hits-the-road in your *CareerRoadmap*. You want to combine names, contacts and opportunities, and a plan for how to follow-up. You could respond to a conference talk or a published article, by writing a letter or sending an email directly to the speaker or author, with your thoughts, comments, and suggestions -- the purpose is to show this person that you know what you are talking about, that you might be easy to work with, and that you bring ideas and knowledge and opportunities to the table. But ***DO NOT*** attach a resume in any first contact, and do not even include a bio within such an initial letter. These contacts don't have to be at a high level within a company that you like. They could be an influential consultant who knows a lot of people and contacts in the industry. Or they could be a person like yourself who is also looking for opportunities. But you must be directed and focused in this follow up and must not waste your time on dead-ends.

Another approach is to write directly to the CEO of a company that you like, and reference a recent timely and important item which affects their company and the industry, and could lead to opportunities for the company -- this is a lead which you will try to leverage to show your skills, experience, and what you can do for the company and especially to help the CEO. Most likely, the actual CEO will never see your letter or respond themselves, but a correspondence secretary might route your letter to someone who would be interested in the company opportunities that you identify. This whole follow-up plan is NOT "throwing mud at the wall to see what sticks" but is a carefully balanced program to build more leads, test the waters, and get ready for the next steps.

- ***Action Programs for Career-Building and Job Search***
By now, you must be getting the gist of the concepts of your *CareerRoadmap* -- both the plan itself and the process for maintaining this plan. Your goals and objectives are not a separate

little "laundry list" but rather are imbedded in specific *Roadmap* categories, with specific dates and tasks for fulfillment. You are not going to do this once and then stop. You are going to make it a way of life, whether you are happy on a current job or between jobs. You are going to be very deliberate and persistent, never panic, always positive. You are going to be highly aware of what is going on in your industry and related other industries. You are going to keep your ear to the ground both internally and externally, and cultivate those who can help you. You are going to always retain and build skills useful outside your immediate situation. You are going to give talks and publish articles (with internal approval), and pursue educational activities and certification and licensing as needed.

The upcoming *STEP 2* of this *Guide* focuses on the many things that you must do to build your career, and will expand on the *Roadmap* details that we have just discussed. But at this point, here is a thought for you: *You will know when you have arrived when you don't have to call anyone to look for opportunities -- people will contact you via voicemail, email, or letter because you are a respected point of knowledge and opportunities in your industry and perhaps also in several related industries.* And it won't really take long to get to this point.

****

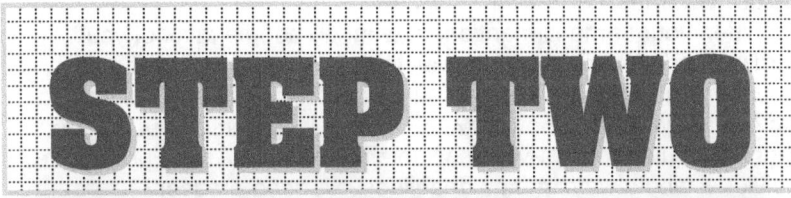

2.1 MANAGING YOUR CURRENT POSITION

Get your act together! You need to have a *plan* for managing your current employment situation -- you should never just "let things happen" and merely react to issues that arise, or merely wait for opportunities that just happen to fall in your lap. Remember -- you are in control of your career and you want it to stay that way.

You not only need a plan, but the plan should have a definite structure and be built around an organized process. You cannot merely build a career plan around a vague notion of your goals in life, but rather you must have a structured process that will keep you up-to-date with current contacts, events, trends, and opportunities.

If you are currently employed, there are a number of things that you need to keep in mind to further your career with your company, or to build a platform from which you can expand to opportunities in other companies.

If you are not working now, or are *under-employed* as are many persons in today's changing global economy, it is extremely important to have a *defined career plan*, plus a *very organized system* to work this plan, and we will cover this in detail further on.

Now, the following are a number of items for which you need to pay close attention in managing your current career position.

• *Your Business Persona*

When your name is mentioned, what do people think of you? A hard worker? A person who is well-liked? A very intelligent and thoughtful individual? A person who gets things done but is hard to like? A leader? An innovator? A good looking person but not too bright? A quiet and not-very-sociable individual? A very productive individual who always meets deadlines? A good dresser?

Or are many people likely to say, "I've seen them in several meetings, and I see them walking around, but I don't know much about them or what they actually do here." Or "They always have something to say in meetings but don't seem to contribute much." Or "This is a very competent individual, who is well liked and could end up being the CEO some day."

How do you think you come across, on the job or on the golf course, or at home? You might even have different personality traits for different situations. But who do you want to be? -- that is the key question. You need to think about this, and to define who you are, and how you come across in your current position, and to think about any improvements needed to align with your career goals. Here are some items to think about:

✓ "People like people who are like themselves" -- meaning pay attention to what Image others project

✓ Many organizations have dress-down Fridays today, and even permit business-casual attire all the time. But each organization will have its own "code of dress," often established by what the CEO and upper management wear. Pay attention to such details.

✓ Check the time at which your boss and management above you arrive in the morning, and be at work even before they arrive.

✓ Decide what colors and clothing styles look the best on you. Don't overdress, and don't under-dress for any particular situation.

✓ Control your business persona carefully -- never a phony, but bulletproof and futureproof.

✓ When meeting someone new, immediately assess their speech and appearance and deal with them accordingly. Always start off pleasant and no-nonsense. Then when you know who you are dealing with, you can respond appropriately. If you know that there might be a problem, still start off pleasantly. You can always fire the big guns later.

- **Position Definition**

It sounds basic, but every position within an organizations must be defined. Namely, what is expected, what are the deliverables, what are the goals and objectives of the position? If a job is not defined, then you know there will be trouble later in evaluating your own performance and outputs. It is amazing that many organizations are filled with people who don't know exactly what is expected of them. Sometimes a boss will every year ask for additional headcount, because they are "busy" and "overloaded," but at the same time they are not required to specifically state exactly what everyone in his or her organization is supposed to do. Such bosses often run an organization on an ad-hoc and short-term basis, maybe even changing and rotating assignments every few days and certainly within a month. It is hard to work in such an organization. To break through this situation, you have to take the initiative and document your assigned tasks and time allocation and constantly inform your boss. But it might be worth the additional overhead if your boss is a key player within the company, and also totally supports you and evaluates you as a top performer.

- **Balance Assignments and Proactive Initiatives**

Even if you are an officer level or CEO of a company, you will still be given assignments by superiors or those to whom you are responsible, like the chairman or the board of directors. But you must balance such assigned items with those items which you initiate yourself. This very much depends on your level and function within the organization. However, every job at every level still leaves room for initiatives. If your position is new and there are no established guidelines, then you should strive to establish a 50-50 balance between things assigned and things that you initiate.

If you merely wait until you are told what to do, you are in danger of several things happening. If you are a good performer and a hard worker, you might soon find that "you have monkeys on your back" -- meaning that every time something comes down the line with a hot deadline, your boss gives the item to you, because he or she knows that you will do it right and get it done on time, even if you have to work through the night. Secondly, your boss might be saving "good assignments" for others in the organization whom he or she favors over you, and be giving you the "junk assignments." He or she might also be giving tasks with high visibility to others, and the "heads-down" mundane assignments to you.

One way to break out of this situation, right in the beginning of a new position, is to take the initiative and propose important tasks immediately - but of course only after thinking everything through initially, including the value not only to your company, but also the value and positioning for your chain of management.

Your overall goal here is to make sure that you write a record of accomplishments, for any position you hold, of which you will be proud, and which does not end up looking like "busywork" or out-of-date legacy work. You want to be able to look back or refer back to any assignments as adding positively to your career, and building on your career path.

- **Build and Nurture Contacts in Your Current Position**
Starting with your immediate line of management, you want to cultivate contacts both through work assignments and any other opportunities that present themselves, such as meetings and teaming activities. You should also plan updates and lunches carefully, with your boss on a regularly scheduled basis, and with others who are influential within your organization. However, be very sensitive to going around your boss or line of management. You want to avoid any situation where a third party would call your boss, referring to a "meeting" which the two of you had held, and your boss was kept in the dark, especially on a subject that could affect him or her directly.

The business of nurturing relationships is very much related to the sales process, and much has been written on the subject. You should devote a concerted and ongoing effort to nurturing relationships. The upcoming *Section 2.4* addresses the building of a great contacts system for your career development.

- **Working a Meeting**
Don't just "take a meeting" -- you must learn to work a meeting to the advantage of your career. If it is your own meeting that you have called, then: (1) Have an agenda, which is agreed-upon by key players ahead of time, and circulated to all attendees well in advance with a meeting announcement. (2) Choose an appropriate meeting

place and venue. If it is an important meeting kicking off a critical project, find an appropriately sized and appointed meeting room, even if you need to get permission to use a specially-reserved executive conference room. If it is an informal status meeting, of course find a small but convenient room. Never have a meeting in an uncomfortable or inconvenient location. (3) Order appropriate refreshments for the meeting, and if budgets or approvals don't permit this, then bring your own refreshments. (4) If slides are to be shown, have the best electronic PC projector and screen available, with a remote control unit. (5) Have any handouts all ready ahead of time and have enough of them. (5) Invite attendees carefully and selectively, and try to get key players. Postpone the meeting if the right decision-makers cannot attend. Target levels above you as appropriate, and always ask your boss if she or he would like to attend. There is no point in having a meeting of merely "message-takers" who cannot speak for their organizations and will just force another meeting to take place on the same subject. (6) The meeting should have a definite goal or multiple goals and objectives. Even just a "discussion meeting" or a "brainstorming session" needs goals, and you must avoid devolving into a "group therapy" session or a "gripe session." (7) If it is your own meeting, you must demonstrate many concurrent qualities -- leadership, organization, interpersonal relations, knowledge, friendliness, persistence, focus, goal-orientation. (8) You must dress and exhibit a comportment both appropriate to the situation and which will further your career.

When you enter a meeting room, make sure that your presence is known. It is good to not arrive alone, but rather with some other key plays, and in a small 3-4 person entourage. Before the meeting, go around the room and introduce yourself to any new or unknown persons. At the beginning of the meeting, go around the table and let everyone introduce themselves, and even ask them to please say a few words about their organization and the relationship to the subject of the meeting. Always have an introduction, and if there are more than ten attendees, stand up, have a warm and friendly introduction using carefully chosen words, emphasize the importance of the subject, and exhibit a no-nonsense presence, but get a sense of the stress level from the body language and statements of the attendees, and be prepared to introduce humor as a tool to reduce stress if necessary.

If higher-level persons or officers are in attendance, make a point of asking for their input, but do not make them uncomfortable or let them take over the meeting. At a break or pre-meeting, mention to them some things about their organization and key issues currently on the table. Emphasize your knowledge-level and understanding of the challenges and solutions.

So, to summarize, every meeting is a benchmark in your career. You want to write a record of accomplishment to which you can refer back as needed. Think of every meeting as a tool to further your career.

- *Manage Office Politics*

  Do not be so naïve as to think that office politics do not matter, and that working smart and working hard is all that matters. If you are in a small company, then everyone knows each other and news travels fast. If you are in a large company, there will be "fiefdoms" and departmental rivalries. Then there are "favorites" and "well connected" employees who might be relatives or friends of persons in high places. There are also office sexual affairs that can affect your own career situation.

  The first thing you must do is to separate company culture and associated office politics with office politics which do not fit within the culture. You must also understand the persona of your management chain and determine if your office persona is in concert with theirs. Make sure you define office persona to include how you look, dress, talk, write, and interact with others. You need to not only fit in well, but at the same time establish a differentiating persona of your own which will further your career.

  One thing that helps in dealing with office politics is to find one or more supporters or angels within the organization. Your angels will be persons of influence within the organization, but who are also altruistic and supportive, and who are friendly to you, and of course persons whom you trust to never undermine your career. They can be a sounding board for helping you with situations that might arise, and will keep matters in confidence.

  If you totally detest the idea of dealing with office politics, then you must find a career situation where you are alone most of the time, like a heads-down programming job or some paperwork or accounting jobs. However, be aware that such jobs are often likely candidates for outsourcing overseas, and might not pay as well as other jobs requiring interpersonal activities and interdependence. It might be a better idea to start for yourself a program to develop your interpersonal skills, or even to consider changing companies to find an environment where the culture and inevitable politics fit your persona.

Some other guidelines regarding company culture:

- ✓ Don't try to confront or resist company culture. This includes the things already discussed, like dress, communication styles, and office hours.

- ✓ It is positive to differentiate yourself and stand above the crowd, but this must be in concert with company culture.

- ✓ Don't expect the business environment to be at all democratic. Don't expect free speech. Don't expect fair decisions. Be prepared for many arbitrary actions.

- ✓ Don't get involved in any office sexual affairs. If you are single, dating peers or co-workers or employees who report to you (or your boss or other management levels above you) has many dangers. If the relationship does not work out, you have created damage which cannot be undone. If the relationship continues over a period of time, it can set you up for "blackmail" if you should want to end the affair, and things could easily spin out of control. If you are married, be loyal to your spouse. Don't envy those who attempt to "sleep their way up" in an organization -- they are always on thin ice and their whole little plan can and often does blow up in their face.

- ✓ Making positive suggestions to strengthen and improve company culture are OK, but remember that there are risks in doing so. You have to know to whom you are talking, and their point-of-view before you start throwing ideas on how to "fix" things from your own perspective.

- ✓ Self-awareness is important – namely how do you come across, what is your self-defined and self-controlled business persona.

- ✓ Your behavior must demonstrate reliability, consistency, control, and a high level of competence. Avoid emotional outbursts and inconsistent behavior. Practice stress management and as needed develop your own personal stress management tools.

✓ Be friendly, open, and approachable in all settings. Say good morning, hello, and don't look away or avoid eye contact. When walking around the halls, carry some papers.

✓ Develop and follow a well-controlled "networking" and contacts development program. *(More on this in Section 2.4)*

✓ Identify and target "angels" and "sponsors" that you think could help your career. But monitor and evaluate these persons. Be careful what you tell them and do not fall into a naïve blind-trust.

✓ "Favorites" within an organization are repulsive to peers, but it is OK for you yourself to become the "favorite" of any influential person, but never a favorite of a person that everybody does not like and who cannot help your career.

✓ Be aware that some jobs and promotions are "hard wired" and that even if you exhibit exceptional qualifications, you might be locked out of an opportunity. On the other hand, you yourself will want to be on track for such a hard-wired opportunity.

✓ In some organizations "games are played" constantly. Two people are hired for the same job, and one will be fired after a surreptitious trial period. They could have two different titles and be located in different places. You want to sense such a situation and to be the survivor.

✓ There will be peers both within and adjacent to your organization who wish to derail you, especially if you are well-positioned and a top performer. You need to build a wall of protection from such persons. Be aware that they will try to steal or misrepresent your ideas, and even plagiarize from your writing and presentations. In addition to security of your own information, you should engender fear on their part, but at the same time always be friendly and courteous.

✓ Hearsay and rumors can be destructive, but also helpful, and very much depend on the source. Don't spread rumors. If you hear some privileged information that is reliable, do not spread this and keep it to yourself, but also decide how you should react or how you can leverage this information to further your own career.

✓ Do not get involved in any illegal behavior related to the company. This includes things like insider trading, conflict of interest, or abuse of company intellectual property. If you find out that somebody in the company is doing something illegal, many companies have an "ethics coordinator" to report activities anonymously and confidentially, or you can talk (confidentially) to the legal department. If you decide bravely to become a "whistle blower," you must be prepared for negative reactions and retaliation, and you must have a lot of persistence, and must have some very solid evidence, not just hearsay.

- ***Managing Your Boss and Your Reporting Staff***
   Your immediate superior is both your manager and your supporter. You want to develop a relationship via which there is an understanding that you will go all-out to support your boss in every circumstance, but that in return you expect that same level of support. Sometimes we are forced to work for a "difficult boss." You need to learn how to manage such a situation. You need to decide what your boos should know and what they should not know. One of the approaches is to become valuable to a number of other organizations, and to creatively develop additional contacts. If your boss is difficult but influential, then you want to work the situation accordingly, demonstrating impeccable competence, a high level of organization, and showing a high level of support for management. But if your boss is difficult but not influential and not liked by anybody else, then your can: (a) work at getting this boss transferred out or fired so that you can take their job, or (b) get out of the organization ASAP.

   For those reporting to you, make sure that they know right from the beginning that you will support them 150% but that you in turn expect them to always support you. Select reporting staff carefully, and let them know that you expect a high level of performance, since you yourself are a top performer. Some people are looking for a safe-and-easy warm spot in an organization, and you don't want to hire such persons. You must foster a high level of loyalty. If you detect conflicts among your reporting staff, deal with such conflicts directly and immediately -- don't let problems grow out of control. Bring them in and make it known they need to work things out as professionals, and that you will not tolerate pettiness and destructive behavior.

- **How To Leave An Organization**

    It is best to leave an organization only when you have found a better opportunity – either a promotion or a situation which you can better leverage to advance your career. But sometimes you might want to leave to get out of a bad situation which you cannot control, like an impossible boss or destructive and antagonistic peers, or an organizational change which has de-positioned your work, or a merger-acquisition that portends trouble. In any case there are several rules to follow:

    ✓ Never "slam-the-door," namely always leave things open such that you might come back if you have to, or if you run into the same boss in the future.

    ✓ Always get references immediately, even if you don't need them at this time. Make it easy for the person you need as a reference, and draft up a complete but short, positive, and powerful reference letter.

    ✓ Make an exit as gracefully as possible, have lunch, talk up good experiences.

    ✓ Keep in touch with supportive, influential, and helpful persons from your past – send emails, keep contact information up-to-date.

- **Choose An Organization Which Fits Your Style**

    Some organizations operate at the "leading-bleeding-edge" – always taking risks, looking for breakthroughs, and absorbing losses along with celebrating successes. In such a situation, usually everybody is a workaholic, and a high level of persistence is hopefully matched by high competence. It can be exciting to work in such an environment, and sometimes when success is reached, everyone becomes a multimillionaire for a short time through an IPO and a "piece of the action." But this environment is not for everyone, and you need to decide what you want and where you fit. People can burn out in such a situation if they are not careful. But others will miss the action and yearn for such an environment if they should leave for something "safer."

If you work in a very stable area of business, make sure that it is truly "futureproof" and not just on the path to being "legacy" and ripe for outsourcing and offshoring. Otherwise you will soon find yourself out on the street, with skills and experience related only to the past and little for the future. One approach in a soon-to-be-legacy area is to pursue training in a related or higher-prospect area while holding on to the supposedly safe position for as long as it lasts. Hopefully your timing and control will work out as you planned.

Tie yourself to important company priorities, and keep up to date on such priorities as they might change. You do not want to find yourself stuck in a position which is at odds with priorities.

Another organizational and personal style preference is generalization versus specialization. If you have both general and also specialized skills this is ideal -- namely you have several areas of special skills, like computers or sales, or technical or financial knowledge, but also have the background, education, and experience to manage broadly. You will then be quite valuable to an organization, and will be sought after when something challenging needs to be accomplished.

- ***Converting Anger to Action***
  There are many circumstances in today's employment environment that can cause you to feel disappointed and angry. Sometimes we encounter a number of negatives in our current position, like dysfunctional management, or misinformation and lack of information on an important subject.

You might have been assigned to a new boss who is not of your choosing, and who presents numerous problems and has to be dealt with carefully. You might have been passed over for a promotion that you thought you deserved, only to see the opening filled by someone of much less experience and capability. Companies sometimes cut job benefits drastically in order to satisfy the bean counters and financial analysts, overruling human resources goals, in disregard of how many people might leave the company and in disregard of the real long-term damage. And you might have been fired or laid off for a variety of reasons: cost-cutting, a merger-acquisition, a mistake that was not your fault, or other reasons that you feel were totally unjustified.

Your task is to convert any anger that you might harbor to *motivation and action* that will not only achieve recovery in your career planning, but also motivate you to move to a new level of opportunity. Sometimes people have left an organization, only to discover that they have talents that they never fully developed before. They often then find a new organization that really appreciates their particular experience, accomplishments, and perspective, and they fully resonate with the new culture and move to a very satisfying career path. Sometimes, they are motivated by a negative event to pursue new training and education, and then also find a much better situation than they ever previously held. And sometimes, individuals have turned around a negative career event and started their own business and flourished way beyond their expectations.

Finally, a few additional pointers on dealing with organizational culture:

- ✓ Keep impeccable records
- ✓ Balance peer-socialization and also managing-up and managing-down
- ✓ Have a "Plan B" for all tasks and for impending organizational changes, including mergers & acquisitions, restructuring, force reductions.
- ✓ "Over-communicate" to avoid misunderstandings, like sending the same information out via fax, email, and in hard copy, especially when dealing internationally across language barriers.
- ✓ Don't "set yourself up" by publishing controversial unresolved items. Things in this category deserve behind-the-scenes treatment.
- ✓ Maintain a professional standing (outside reputation) as well as an internal organizational standing, but without conflicts of interest or conflicts in loyalties.

Now enough on the subject of company culture and things to avoid, and on to a positive outlook of you yourself developing career opportunities.

****

2.2 DEVELOPING YOUR CAREER BUSINESS PLAN

A business plan is a document that is needed to advocate any proposed venture or a new line of business for an existing entity. Your career is at least as important as any particular venture, and deserves the same business plan treatment, to help you in organizing and managing your career, but keeping it concise and to the point. In a traditional business plan, there is great attention paid to a business case and related spreadsheet numbers. Going along with these numbers is a complete description of the venture, its goals and objectives, and many related assumptions, background, and often market research information.

Why do you need a *Career Business Plan*? First of all, to concisely organize your career planning and development, and also to reinforce for yourself the goals, objectives, and the "return on investment" that you will receive over your lifetime for proactively developing your career. Nobody would undertake a venture and "play it by ear" and let events control the venture, but many people do exactly this when it comes to management of their own career.

- **Elements of a Career Business Plan**
  You do not need to make your *Career Business Plan* a voluminous document. Rather, you should make it concise, to the point, and keep it up to date. Here are the major elements that you should include in the *Career Business Plan*:

  ✓ **Career Goals**
  A career goal will vary with the individual. (*Section 1* of this *Guide* went into great detail on the subject of career planning and career goals.) A short term goal might be to move up one or two levels within an organization, or to achieve a particular certification or licensing level, or to obtain a particular degree, or reach a certain level of compensation, or to take steps toward starting a business of your own. Long term goals might include reaching officer-level or CEO level within a company, or achieving tenure or department head level within an academic institution, or becoming a full partner within a professional practice, or growing your own business to a defined level. The point is that at the beginning of your *Career Business Plan* you must document your goals and objectives. If you cannot do this, you need to go back to career planning and decide what you want to do with your life and career.

✓ *Career Objectives*

The objectives for your career will detail and support your career goals. Objectives must have timeframes associated and be measurable. Example: For a goal of moving up a level in an organization, you must set objectives like demonstrating and achieving outstanding performance ratings, fully understanding the requirements of the next level in your own or an associated organization, identifying persons whom you need to cultivate and how and when, establishing mentors and "angels" who can help, and so forth. For someone whose goal is to change fields, their objectives must detail what education and training that they will require, how they will develop contacts needed, what career information that they must gather, and how they will identify and evaluate career opportunities in the new field. *(Later in this Step 2, there are Sections which will tell you how to develop your Career Information System, Your Career Contacts System, and Your Career Opportunities System.)*

✓ *Career Earnings Forecast and a Lifetime Financial View*

There is nothing like putting numbers on a particular item. Trying to quantify something forces us to think about things and trying to forecast numbers forces us to think about and plan the future, and to make assumptions about the future. When you first draft your *Career Business Plan*, you might not have any idea what your earnings will be over your lifetime, so you might initially want to leave blank any spreadsheet for your career earnings until you set up the bulk of your **Career Planning System**, which is detailed in the upcoming *Sections*. However, it is useful to *force yourself* to think about how much you will earn over your career and what your earning goals are and what assumptions about your life and career you need to make. Doing this will bring up choices that you need to make, and information that you need to gather, and realities that must be dealt with, and can make people wake up and make decisions that they have refused to face.

There are important considerations involved in attempting to forecast a lifetime income statement and balance sheet. First of all, you will realize that maintaining merely one stream of revenue over your lifetime is virtually impossible, and is not desirable. Staying in the exact same job forever (50+ years) is not going to happen, so you need to think about various career paths, compensation alternatives, and multiple streams of revenue. You also need to think of expenses on your lifetime income statement, and of a balance sheet of assets and liabilities over your lifetime.

It is OK to set goals for your future earnings, but do not be driven into useless speculation about income, assets, and liabilities, and do not make any unrealistic projections of these numbers. But rather, identify what goes behind the numbers, namely career choices, lifestyle choices, and what you will need to do over your lifetime to define yourself and to reach the career market value for which you are aiming.

✓ ***Career Business Case Alternatives***
An important aspect of a career business plan is identifying and documenting alternative career paths and choices. You cannot control everything in your life or in a particular career position, but the important thing is for you to be proactive and have plans to control as much as you can in your life.

Sometimes individuals will deliberately plan ahead to change career paths at a particular point in their lives. For example, some people will want to work in a profession for a number of years, and then change to teaching at a particular time, perhaps after their children graduate from college. Some persons have deliberately had a career in the military and then retired from the military and started a second career in a particular company, with the intention of then retiring from that company and having a second pension. Others might deliberately plan to work in a particular country for a period of time and then work in another country or return to their native country. Still others will deliberately plan to work in a particular capacity and then return to school to learn another skill and transition to another career position.

You need to include alternatives in your *Career Business Plan*, and as you go through this *Guide* you will develop ideas about what these alternatives should be for your unique persona, capabilities, experience, and perspective.

✓ Contingency Planning for Your Career Business Plan

Beyond planned-for alternative career paths in your *Plan*, you need to think about career contingency events, namely things that you did not plan on happening. Even the best plans must face unknowns and the realities of the global economy, the whims of dysfunctional management, and the bean-counter mentality found in many organizations. *(Sections 2.7, 2.8, and 2.9 of this Guide address contingency planning for your career.)* These unknowns are one of the reasons that you must strive for control of your own career, be very proactive about career planning, and maintain skills, contacts, and an awareness of career opportunities. When you first draft your *Career Business Plan*, you will not have a full awareness of contingencies, but by the time you get your *Career Opportunity System* in place, you should be well prepared to deal with unknowns.

This closes the subject of your *Career Business Plan*. The next section of this *Guide* will now start you on the process of building your own *Career Opportunity System*, starting with a *Career Information System*.

****

2.3 BUILDING A CAREER INFORMATION SYSTEM

In *Section 1.6*, one of the important elements of your **Career Roadmap** was information development – defined as *"...a well-organized system, primarily electronic databases including downloads, email, and other stored file systems and databases, for all information that will help drive your career planning. "* In short, you will never be able to get control of your career if you do not get highly organized so that you will never miss out on a real career opportunity.

In this section, we will expand on the idea of a career information system, as mentioned in the *Career Roadmap Section*. Your *Career Information System* will then define a firm basis for your planning and control activities.

First, try to get as much information as possible into an electronic form. This way, you can store and then quickly access the information in a variety of ways. You can automatically feed your *Career Information System* using RSS (Really Simple Syndication) feeds from many websites. See the *Appendix* section on RSS to help you set this up. You can also opt-in to websites to have email items of interest sent to you. And you can set up for search engine results to automatically be sent to your email address, via Google Alerts and other search capabilities.

On the next page is a diagram of the elements of your *Career Information System.*

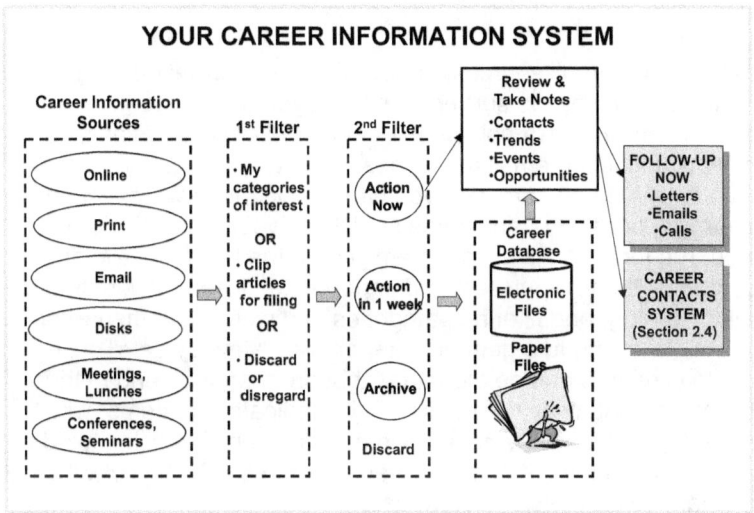

When you are first setting up your *Career Information System*, keep in mind that this is a very important factor in your life, and therefore you should adhere to a number of specific steps, including the following:

- Create one or more *new email addresses*, named appropriately, on sites such as Google and Yahoo. These new email addresses will be dedicated to your career management process. Other existing email addresses might be involved, but you will want to avoid co-mingling of any other personal and certainly company email information. Also, keep in mind the highest security regarding any email, and have an email information backup plan.

- *Outgoing* email related to your career activities presents many security dangers, so treat outgoing email very carefully, and invest time in the beginning for learning about email security and to acquire email security software accordingly.

- For the new email addresses that you create solely and exclusively for career management, you must set up numerous folders, appropriately named to organize the incoming email that you will receive related to your career system.

- In addition to email folders, create new career-related folders on a hard drive and also on backup media such as CD-ROM or memory sticks.

Regarding email sources for your *Career Information System*, there are many ways to sort email so that you will not be overwhelmed. For example, in the popular Microsoft Outlook, you can "view" incoming email messages many ways -- by date received, by subject, etc., and you can specify "filter words" such as "career," "opportunity," and items specific to your field. Once you set this up, run through all incoming email over the last few days and then identify items or interest and importance. Keep track of these viewing, sorting, and filtering categories and words, but then return your email viewing to a generic category like "view by date" only. Learn to eliminate and delete things that are marginal, and to then move email right away to "folders" which indicate "hot items" which require immediate follow up, and "interesting items" which should be dealt with within the week, and "reference items" which you will save and database for possible future use.

Another major feed for your *Career Information System* will be from online Internet sources. You will want to automate searches as much as possible, and to be *extremely organized.* Do not fall into the mindless trap of "surfing" the web for "interesting job or career information." And keep away from job posting sites - these are NOT sources of information for your career planning, and will merely chew up your valuable time.

RSS (Really Simple Syndication) is a web methodology that you can use to setup automatic feeds to your email. (If you are not familiar with RSS and RSS Readers, go to the web and search on the topic "RSS.") Also, most of the search engines permit one to set up automatic "alerts" for new items for which search words have been pre-profiled. And of course, "opt in" at key websites will direct information to the email address(s) which you register at those sites. Just a caution: Do not get so absorbed in information-gathering and sorting software and tools that you lose track of your *Career Information System* objective - namely to constantly gather timely information which will assist your career planning, and identification of career contacts and opportunities.

You will also need to keep many paper records for your career management and planning. First, when you get started, either dedicate an entirely new filing cabinet for career items, or at least one full drawer in an existing filing cabinet. For low-cost budgeting, merely use one of the open plastic filing crates available at office supply stores. Buy several boxes of hanging folders with labels to get your paper career filing system off to a very organized start.

60

Regarding paper career-related magazines, keep back issues of publications for a limited time period, but in an organized filing system. Also, do not be afraid to tear a magazine apart and to keep only articles of key importance. If you can subscribe to electronic versions of a paper journal or magazine, you should do so. Otherwise, consider scanning a paper item into an image file, or even faxing it to your computer, so that you can save an image as an incoming fax.

The main point of the above diagram is to get you on a well-defined path to an organized system for supporting your career planning, and control of your life. This is not just a one-time exercise, but rather an ongoing living process. Note that mobile communications (smartphone, WiFi, tablet, etc.) have not been superimposed on this system, but should be an important part of the process as applicable.

The preceding diagram of your *Career Information System* is just a guideline, and everybody will want to put their own spin on how they collect and organize information critical to their career. The objective is to not miss anything important that could help or impede your career, and especially lead to identification of new opportunities and contacts. Of course, the Internet is clearly the world's information network and is highly important, but don't let it become a preoccupation, to the exclusion of a lot of other information sources, such as print and face-to-face sources.

You must be an avid reader and absorber of both internal and external information, both in print, online, through personal contacts, conferences, presentations, and meetings. But you must manage your time carefully, and not read everything you see. You must be very organized in dealing with information, and avoid "information overload."

When you go to a trade show, attend a career fair, read a trade publication, travel, or in fact read any newspaper or magazine, or meet others at meetings and parties, you do not want to just do so for casual or entertainment purposes, although that is an important element of your life. You need to get yourself in an "opportunities attitude" that keeps you alert to possible situations that can benefit your career and your life. You need to sharpen your skills in sizing up people, and not "grilling them" but rather diplomatically and quickly identifying if they can help your career or might even know someone else who can help you. You also need to know how to recognize events (identified online or in print) that could impact you positively or negatively, or can be leveraged in some way. So sharpen your sources, keep them up to date, and be flexible in bringing on any new sources that you identify.

There are two steps that you need to take in boiling-down career information. First, you need to get electronic information into a proper file system, and also file and index paper information so that you can come back to it quickly and efficiently. And importantly, you need to discard anything that is neither important at this time, or that you deem will not be important in the future.

Next, you need to filter the remaining information for actions NOW, in 1 week, or for your archives. And at this second stage, you need to discard more items, after giving them a second review.

Out of this second career information filter, you need to identify contacts (names, titles, organizations, email or telephone or physical address); events & trends (what, where, who, when); and through your own judgment, list possible career opportunities. The contacts can go into *Your Career Contacts System* (see the next *Section 2.4*). And you can then begin to consider follow-up actions for the important items that you have identified as NOW items. Depending on what information that you have available, you could send a letter, an email, or a voicemail. But at this early stage, you want to be very careful about what you do. (More about managing contacts later.)

Suggested Career Information Database Structure

In many cases, you will want to use an electronic platform for your *Career Information System* that is either a spreadsheet (for example Excel) or a relational database (for example Access) for the *Career Database* indicated as a drum in the previous diagram. You could also merely use a word processor program, but linking items together could be cumbersome. This structure is something which only you yourself can devise, and is highly related to your personal perspective, occupational field(s), and goals. But, here is an *example* structure, based on a spreadsheet platform.

Career Information System Workbook #1: Basic Information

- *Spreadsheet #1*: Economic segment(s): e.g., medical, mining, computers, communications, services, consulting, marketing, carpentry, plumbing, engineering, law, dentistry, teaching, government, religion, finance, ...

- *Spreadsheet #2: (linked to Spreadsheet#1):* Economic sub-segment(s): e.g., cardiovascular, seismology, oil drilling, PC operating systems, smartphone apps, retail store management, time management consulting, ad campaign design, new home framing, commercial HVAC, circuit design, contract law, dental surgery, secondary math instruction, local government zoning administration, pastoral guidance, investment banking, ...

- *Spreadsheet #3: (linked appropriately):* Regulatory, Legislative, Licensing, Professional Rules

- *Spreadsheet #4: (linked appropriately):* Educational, training, certification, licensing information

- *Spreadsheet #5: (linked to Spreadsheet#2):* Online website links and excerpts and abstracts and your own comments and notes from articles, images, pages, etc.

- *Spreadsheet #6: (linked to spreadsheet#3);* Trends identified, contacts identified, companies identified, other organizational entities identified, events identified, opportunities identified (all of these with dates associated)

Career Information System Workbook #2: Electronic Articles, Various Full Content Items *(with links for all of the following spreadsheets)*

- *Spreadsheet #1:* Full electronic text of articles

- *Spreadsheet #2:* White Papers

- *Spreadsheet #3:* Particular Tables, Images of Importance

Career Information System Workbook #3: Hot Items; Your Own Reactions, Notes, Initial Implications for Your Career *(with links for all of the following spreadsheets)*

- *Spreadsheet #1*: Hot contacts, your own review comments, follow-up for these, including timing, media for follow ups

- *Spreadsheet #2*: Hot topics, trends, how you will monitor, publications and links and other sources to monitor for changes and career opportunities

- *Spreadsheet #3*: Things to avoid, warnings, security concerns, conflicts

Lastly, here are a few examples of career information situations:

- You are scanning a trade magazine and you see an article written by an officer-level or influential person in an organization that you respect, and on a topic on which you have both knowledge and experience. As you are going through the article, you are thinking about and jotting down how you might possibly contact this person, to start a dialog about the subject, and about opportunities that will be opening up in the industry. Sometimes an article will have a short biography at the end of the article, identifying contact information, including even an email address. Alternatively, you can always write to the editor, asking that your comments be forwarded to the author. When you finish reading the article, you will be in a good position to draft your comments to this person, but you do not want to "shoot from the hip" and rather will want to carefully consider your possible response, if any, to the article. Your objective is to further your career via such a contact. You do NOT ever at this point want to ever attach a resume, or ask about job openings. Your objective is to cultivate a contact.

- You are walking the floor of a trade show and go into the booth of a company which you already know is a key player in the industry. You judicially spot an officer of the company and discretely join a discussion that is underway, and at the appropriate time pass your business card and introduce yourself. If it is appropriate, you initiate a dialog on their products and services, and the opportunities ahead, and you obtain identifying information on this person and others. You end this dialog by thanking for your discussion and closing on a positive statement of opportunities. Then you move to a private spot to jot down the contact information and you outline what actions your are going to take, if any, to possibly follow-up.

- While going through your daily information sources, you see reference to an important upcoming conference or seminar, in an area in which you either have experience and knowledge, or an interest as a possible career path. You follow up by checking other sources to obtain an agenda, a brochure, and a list of speakers. Whether you actually attend or not, you track this event to see what develops, and perhaps obtain related documents and reviews. At a minimum, you make sure that you are maintaining your current expertise, or developing new areas of expertise.

- At a career fair, the human resources representatives that are sent there to staff a booth usually just want to collect resumes, and do quick face-to-face assessments. They might not have any real jobs open, or they might be selectively screening persons to come in a few days later to an event where they can do the next stage of evaluation. They almost certainly will not be actual hiring managers themselves, and usually will not be very knowledgeable about the company's actual operations, financial situation, or hottest products and services, much less opportunities ahead for the industry. So if you do choose to spend some of your valuable time at a career fair, use it to get information about a company that you respect. But remember, you might get more out of merely going to their website or reading their annual report.

- If on an airplane ride or sitting at a bar you per-chance happen to bump into someone who works at a company that you have been tracking, and you offer your own business card and contact information, and try to get the same from them. See if you can get them to give insights about the company, or (non-proprietary) information about future opportunities and offerings in the pipeline. In such situations, it might help to have a card without your company identification, and even with a proxy name or alias. But be aware of security concerns and problems that you will have in following up with your real identification.

****

2.4 BUILDING YOUR CAREER CONTACTS AND CONNECTIONS SYSTEM

One of the most important steps that you can take is to set up a *System* for keeping track of, and cultivating, contacts and connections in your life and in one or more industries, governmental, or academic areas. You MUST have a complete

Contact System for doing this, not just names scribbled on paper and piled or filed away. If you send out letters or emails without a system, you could not only lose control of the situation quickly, but you are in danger of irretrievably messing up career contacts, and missing out on some real opportunities. .

By definition, a *career contact* is a person, and a *career connection* is an organization or a relationship that can possibly be utilized to open a career opportunity. Connections could be through family or friends, professional associates, past employment, through associations or academic institutions. For example, the fact that you attended a particular school or college or training institute will remain a connection for life. If you hear about activities associated with these, you have the option of contacting them and inquiring in a manner that might lead to particular contacts and career opportunities. Likewise, if someone in your family works at a particular professional organization (law firm, medical facility or medical practice, accounting firm, consulting firm, partnership) or at a particular private company or at a particular governmental agency, then this is a connection which you can utilize in the proper manner to possibly identify particular contacts and career opportunities.

The following diagram will help you develop your own *Career Contacts and Connections System.*

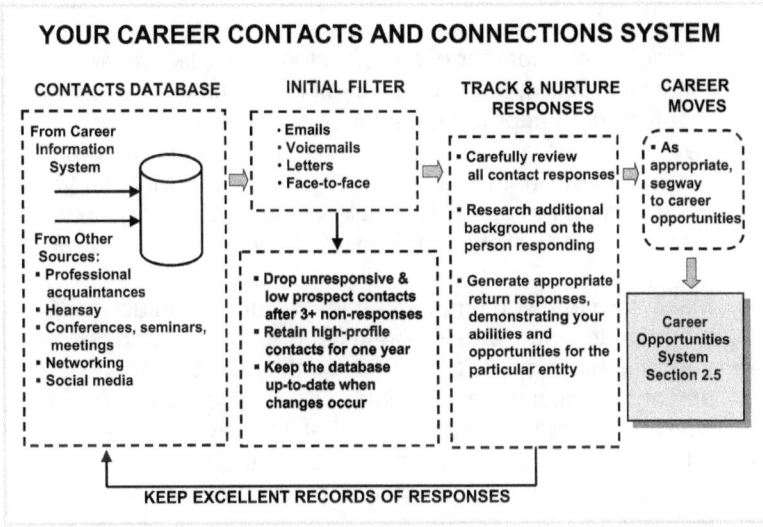

YOUR CAREER CONTACTS AND CONNECTIONS SYSTEM

- **First,** you need to establish a wide range of *sources* for contacts and connections. Of course, the *Career Information System* described in *Section 2.2* will be one major source of these contacts. You will include names that you see in articles of interest, speakers at conferences, online names, business cards collected at trade shows and meetings, newspaper items with names, names mentioned by colleagues, names from courses and seminars, and of course names from current and prior employment situations. Not only do you want to develop such a list, but you also need a disciplined process for obtaining contacts. Make sure that the process fits your own style and situation. Keep as many details about each contact as possible -- even things like their family, hobbies, and interests, and what you remember about them, last contact, how you found their name, and their title and organization. Included in the *Appendix* are links to identify conventions, trade groups, and publications that will be sources for career contacts.

- A *career connection* is not necessarily a particular person, and sometimes the connection is a particular entity like a company, department, or association. Again, if you are an alumnus of a particular educational entity, the entity itself is a connection, and within that entity you might have many contacts, and will be eligible to utilize the alumni association and its various resources to further your career appropriately. Likewise, if a deceased member of your family was a distinguished member of a professional firm, like a law firm or medical practice, then you yourself might make reference to that firm in an appropriate manner. Companies where you have worked are a connection, even if there is nobody in particular left whom you previously knew. The fact that you once worked there, and hopefully established a very positive record of accomplishment, is itself of value for your career.

- Make sure that you understand that a career contact is *NOT* a person to whom you intend to send a resume, or ask about current job openings, or even ask if they have heard about any organizations that are hiring. Your major initial goal is to cultivate a relationship, to show that you have ideas and unique knowledge in an industry, to get their feedback on particular events, and to determine their professional persona.

- Don't pass up any opportunity to establish contacts. At a meeting, either internal or external to a current career situation, always get the name, title, organization, and contact information for each attendee. When you go to a trade show or conference, keep track of the names of all speakers, and if you have heard their talks, take notes and keep these on file, and try to get contact information for as many as possible. Immediately assess the importance of any such contacts for furthering your career, and draft ideas for following up to nurture a potential contact and to evaluate that contact.

- When you have established your own (highly protected) list of contacts, and "certified" them as persons who have influence and knowledge and are reliable and sincere, and can be trusted for confidentiality -- only then will you consider them for exploring career opportunities, and then in an indirect and managed way.

- Note that we are *not* talking here about setting up a "networking group" for merely a job search. Often this is a waste of time, and devolves into a bunch of people chasing job openings and hearsay, or providing group therapy for each other, or calling people from years ago who don't even remember who you are. You can use up a lot of time on such activities, including meetings, phone calls, emails and blogs -- valuable time that you can devote to a positive and proactive action plan.

- **Secondly,** you need to establish an excellent record-keeping system for these sources. A file of business cards might seem helpful, but for each of these you need to write identifying information on the back. The best approach is to setup a database, or just an Excel spreadsheet with contact names, or some other contact list as on a Blackberry smartphone or in Microsoft Outlook, and so forth. Your records should be easily accessible, and you should be able to sort the names many ways, and of course keep the records up-to-date.

  You must categorize contacts, not just lump them all together. Some will be much more important than others, and require more attention and nurturing. Some will be new and untested and unqualified. Some contacts will be quite old and if they have nor responded to your initiatives, they should be generally purged from your *Career System*, depending on your judgment regarding importance.

- **Third,** you need a *process* for cultivating, filtering, and working the contacts. For example, when you see an article of interest related to your career goals, send off an email, letter or note (through the publisher if necessary for forwarding) with your comments. Make sure that whatever you say shows that you are active in the industry, and be careful in making judgmental statements since you don't know the full perspective of this person. But your goal is to get a response, and get a direct address, or even an email address and telephone number, so that in the future you can use this contact.

- After you have had feedback from a contact, you will get to know with whom you are dealing. If they have ideas about industry opportunities, events, and developments, you will know that you have found a useful source of information. Keep in touch with such persons, maybe even send off holiday greetings.

- Keep your contacts private and secure, and don't share your contacts with anyone, not even friends.

- **Fourth,** you must keep your *Career Contacts System* up to date. If addresses, telephone numbers, email addresses,

69

organizations, and job titles change, you do not want to be sending information to an old location, which might get into the wrong hands. Check Linkedin, Facebook, AnyWho, MSN white pages, and a number of other sources in order to keep up to date.

- ***Eventual Career Follow-ups:*** Eventually, you might want to send a "career opportunity" letter to some of your own private contacts that you have previously cultivated. You could mention that you are considering a career move because of your unique experience and some changes in the industry, and would welcome their advise on who might be interested in your background. Don't attach a resume at this point, and don't make it look like you are "searching for a job."

Suggested Career Contacts and Connections Database Structure

As was suggested in *Section 2.3* for your *Career Information System*, you need to establish a well-defined electronic database for career contacts and connections, as depicted as the database drum in the above diagram. Your can parallel the workbook and worksheet suggestions of the *Career Information System*, and make sure that you have many links to other sources and files. Here are some guidelines:

- Always make sure that you document how you identified a contact, namely the date, and circumstances.

- Of course you will list as much fundamental data about each contact, including name, title, organization, physical address, email, phone numbers, fax. This list will grow as you follow-up and nurture a contact. For example, when all you have is the name of the author of an article, you might send a follow-up note to the editor of the publication, requesting that your comments be forwarded to the author. Then, if the author responds to your own contact information, you will begin to build proprietary information to further qualify this contact, and then you will add such information to your *Career Contacts Database*.

- You can "Google" the contact name online, and also check Facebook, Linkedin, etc. to see if there is anything additional available, and then have a section in the *Contacts Database* for this.

- You will have a separate workbook for anything you send out to a contact, as well as any responses. This will be highly organized with date, time, and a full record. You will **never** just send off an exploratory note to a potential contact to "see what happens," only to lose track of what you stated, and then if there is a response months later end up in an embarrassing situation.

- You will have a separate workbook on your strategy for nurturing each contact, with this strategy appropriate to the level, title, and importance of the contact. The strategy will include how you intend to "qualify" the contact and what has worked and what has not worked, and how you will manage each situation and the timing for the contact management.

One additional final thought. It has been said that there are three categories of human traits regarding personal interaction: Independence, codependence, and interdependence. Overly "Independent" people claim that they don't need others and in fact that other people just get in their way. Overly "codependent" people cannot make a decision or decide on a course of action without consulting with many others for every step, and often become stuck in equivocation and over-analysis of an issue. And "Interdependent" people recognize that although we are all separate individuals, our existence and development in life is intertwined with others, and that the effectiveness of our social interaction is an important element in determining our success.

Think of your career contacts and connections as a "team" working together to achieve mutual goals. Don't merely think of contacts as persons that you can lean on and use or even manipulate to further your career. Instead, think of a two-way relationship, in which you bring your experience, knowledge, and perspectives to play in constructive interactions with these contacts. Think of "win-win" situations with your contacts.

****

2.5 DEVELOPING YOUR CAREER OPPORTUNITIES SYSTEM

Having set up both your *Career Information System* and your *Career Contacts System*, you are now ready to consider your system for *Career Opportunities Awareness and Development*.

Both internally and externally, you need to remain constantly aware of career opportunities. But this does not mean checking online job postings all the time. Nor does it mean that you need to constantly ask peers and management above you about open job possibilities. There are a number of Sections below which will help you build your lifetime career development system, and you will see that job ads and online postings are not a recommended primary source for career opportunities.

What you do need to set up is an organized system for keeping your ear to the ground. This includes establishing yourself as a highly visible and highly active member of your current company, as well as within your chosen industry sector. For example, if you find out that some new regulation or legislation will open up opportunities for your company, you need to know how to diplomatically inquire what the company plans to do, and even become an advocate for a proactive direction. If you learn of a newly created division within your current company, you need to assess how this might affect your own position, and whether there will be new opportunities opening up within the company. If you hear of a newly hired senior executive, you need to find out what they will be doing, and whether there might be new opportunities as a result of this change, or conversely if this might mean that there will be a reorganization or a force reduction.

Budget your time carefully for this awareness and opportunities development part of your career plan. You do not want to waste time on hearsay rumors or speculative activities, but rather always be aware of alternative career paths and opportunities. The Internet is a great global information system, but is also full of incorrect information and deliberately misleading comments and blogs. Depend only on reliable sources, and double-check your information.

This information gathering and awareness will help you in the management of your current position, as was reviewed back in *Section 2.1*. If you are both a knowledgeable and reliable source of company and industry information, your peers, your reporting employees, and those superior in the organization will recognize this and refer to you. But be careful -- just one wrong item could spoil your image and derail your career.

You can go online and subscribe to as many e-zines, email opt-ins, and complimentary paper subscriptions as makes sense for your position and industry activities. But don't overload yourself to the point that it impacts your performance and your career planning time management.

You should build a list of "search topics" which you regularly enter into the online search engines, some of these even daily. Strive to be the first in your organization to know of a new event, and then diplomatically and strategically send out emails making reference to this event or item.

Now to organize all of this effort on career opportunities, you need to set up your own *Career Opportunities System*, as depicted in the diagram below.

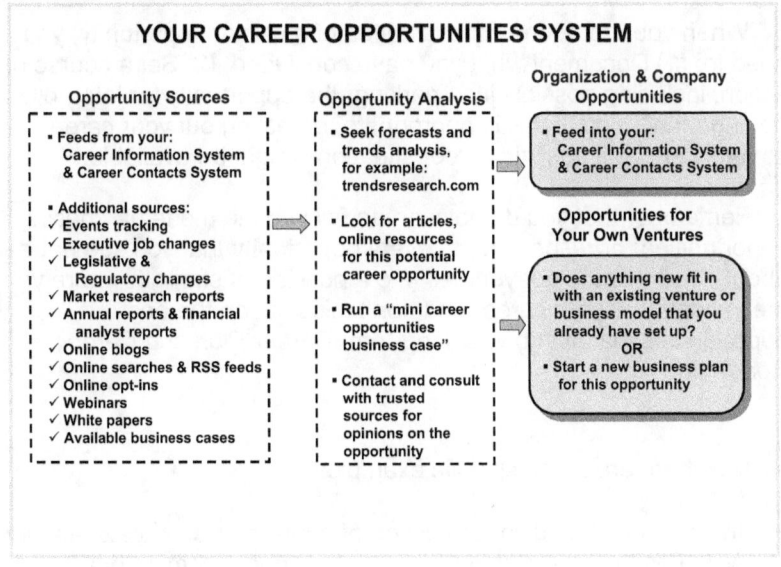

YOUR CAREER OPPORTUNITIES SYSTEM

Opportunity Sources

- Feeds from your:
  Career Information System
  & Career Contacts System

- Additional sources:
  ✓ Events tracking
  ✓ Executive job changes
  ✓ Legislative &
     Regulatory changes
  ✓ Market research reports
  ✓ Annual reports & financial
     analyst reports
  ✓ Online blogs
  ✓ Online searches & RSS feeds
  ✓ Online opt-ins
  ✓ Webinars
  ✓ White papers
  ✓ Available business cases

Opportunity Analysis

- Seek forecasts and
  trends analysis,
  for example:
  trendsresearch.com

- Look for articles,
  online resources
  for this potential
  career opportunity

- Run a "mini career
  opportunities
  business case"

- Contact and consult
  with trusted
  sources for
  opinions on the
  opportunity

Organization & Company Opportunities

- Feed into your:
  Career Information System
  & Career Contacts System

**Opportunities for
Your Own Ventures**

- Does anything new fit in
  with an existing venture or
  business model that you
  already have set up?
  OR
- Start a new business plan
  for this opportunity

73

This idea of keeping a separate system for career opportunities might seem redundant to some readers, having just reviewed previously both your *Career Information System* and your *Career Contacts System*. But it is important for you to keep a log of both short term specific opportunities, and longer-term "futureproof" opportunities. An example of the latter might be environmental-related or energy-related or medical opportunities.

Take a look at the steps in the above diagram. Career opportunity sources that are listed in the first box on the left include just about everything you can name, and of course much might come from your *Career Information* and *Career Contacts Systems*. The second step indicated above requires a little more in-depth analysis than just filtering of information. For example, you want to seek forecasts and projections related to a supposed opportunity, to make sure that if you change career paths or jobs assignments that you are avoiding any area that is predicted to go downhill quickly. In addition, it is useful to do a "back-of-the-envelope" business case on a potential career opportunity. And lastly, you should consult some of your *Career Contact* sources, and see what they think about opportunities in a potential career area that you are considering, but this should be done in a discreet manner, and definitely without any "job-seeking" tone.

When you are done with evaluation of a career opportunity, you need to: (1) Document what you have concluded, (2) Set a course of action, including possibly just "parking" the opportunity for later follow-up and monitoring, if this is appropriate, or testing out your career contacts to see if specific career situations might be available.

Remember that you do not want to fall into the mode of "chasing opportunities" or responding to every opportunity that you see or hear about. You want to get yourself into a position of strength where you are in control of your career and don't miss out on the best opportunities that fit into your long-term *Career Plan* and *Career Roadmap*.

Now here are some specific examples:

* In scanning the business section of newspapers, magazines, and websites that you monitor, you see an announcement of a potential new business venture among several influential partners, in an area where you have some experience and

knowledge and capabilities. You need to flag this as something to monitor closely, and even before such a venture might be actually formed and initiated, you will want to explore possibly getting in early in a key position.

- You notice that several business leaders, and even political leaders, have just met and stated that a particular area is of high importance for future business activities and future economic growth. You need to dig deeper beyond any general or vague publicity to see if this is truly going someplace, including being proactive if you have specific experience and knowledge and insights, and draft an action plan and consult your contacts and-or cultivate new contacts, as appropriate.

- You hear of a new contract being awarded to a company for which you have high regard (not just a buzz-word marquis firm), and you also notice several ads for positions, and check their website and see job posts. It might be late in the process for a real career opportunity at this point, but when companies start hiring they will need experienced managers and officer-level persons to control the activity and to meet objectives. Be cautious, but check this type of situation promptly.

- Usually you want to avoid "turn-around" situations, but if you notice an event such as bringing in a new officer or CEO to fix a bad situation, your might want to analyze this and then respond in an appropriate manner if you have the experience, knowledge, and capabilities to make the turn-around successful, and therefore have a positive element on your resume. But of course, if the turn-around fails, you will have a "Titanic event" on your resume.

****

2.6 THE IMPORTANCE OF YOUR CAREER MARKETING PLAN

So far, we've talked about a lot of information-intensive elements of your overall career planning. But equally important is building and maintaining a career marketing and public relations program (including promotion and awareness) for yourself. It has been said that *"build a better mousetrap and the world will beat a path to your door"* but this has been proven to be a total fallacy. There are many employees who do a great job, sitting in the corner working diligently, but often nobody knows what they are doing, and  they are not considered for any career opportunities. Then there are the employees who actually do very little, try to steal and borrow ideas from others, but make a big deal about everything they do, and make sure that all levels of management learn of their supposed accomplishments. They are spin masters and you need to know how to deal with them. Often, their true reputation will catch up with them, but they can go a long way with very little on the ball.

You want to be a person who is proud of your real accomplishments, who does not try to take credit for the work of others, but is able to easily deflect any erroneous and deliberately misleading information spewed out by jealous rivals. To protect your reputation and presence within an organization, you have to make your own public relations program part of your career planning. In today's online world, many online searches of individual names are conducted, so your online presence is important, as well as maintenance and security of your "online reputation."

You have to develop a mix of both internal and external publicity. If you are a member of an outside industry organization and they have meetings and public relations releases, make sure that you take advantage of any opportunity for your name and/or picture to appear in such releases, even if such releases are just local in nature. If there is an internal company publication, consider getting your name in print, or ask the editor if they would be interested in a story covering something in which you have a direct involvement, and even offer to write up a draft to help them get something in print. And if you do so, you'll make sure that your name and accomplishments are mentioned, and maybe even your picture is included in the article.

76

The whole idea is that *you are in control* of this PR process. You need to build and maintain a *Career Public Relations Process*, as depicted in the diagram that follows.

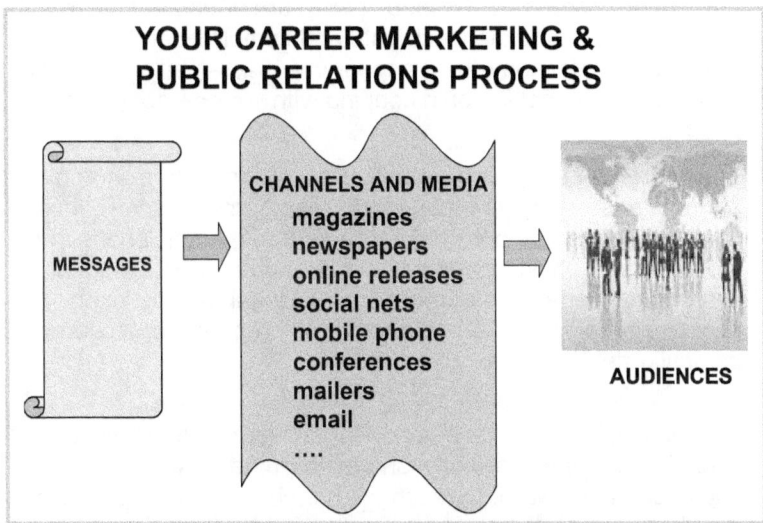

YOUR CAREER MARKETING & PUBLIC RELATIONS PROCESS

MESSAGES

CHANNELS AND MEDIA
magazines
newspapers
online releases
social nets
mobile phone
conferences
mailers
email
....

AUDIENCES

- The messages that you want to publicize are paramount. But you must be extremely careful. Once you tell the world something, especially electronically, a record will exist for a long time, and indelible impressions will have been made.

- An holistic and coordinated approach needs to be maintained in your career public relations program. That is, a powerful and consistent personal brand and image must be coordinated across all media and venues. Email, social network postings, letters, announcements, handouts, brochures, bios associated with articles and talks -- all must project a uniform and consistent message.

- A message can simply be an announcement of something, such as: The publication of an article; giving a presentation at a conference; completion of a program; the attainment of a certification or license; the awarding of a degree; the completion of a construction project; an installation at a particular location or facility; an upcoming artistic performance; changing employment; a job promotion; the start of or completion of a travel program;

participation in a research program or team activity or task force; attainment of governmental approval; and so forth.

- When you present at a conference and are listed in the brochure and agenda for the conference, make sure ahead of time that the information is completely accurate and complete, and to your liking. Do not let something appear in a mass-mailing or online announcement that is not in keeping with your career goals.

- The content of the message should always include a short bio, and make reference to other accomplishments. It should include contact information, possibly a web address, email, phone and mobile, and a physical address if appropriate. Sometimes a student message will state that the individual has just been awarded a particular degree and is well prepared for a career in a particular field.

- The *channels, media, and venue* for delivery of the message should be targeted carefully, and appropriate for the intended audience. If you want to reach the members of your profession, then both a printed, e-zine, and online publication of the trade group or society is appropriate. If you want to reach all alumni of a college that you have attended, then their electronic and print publications will be appropriate. If you want to reach those within your company or institution, then their internal newsletters and company PR department are appropriate. But often, of course, you will want to orchestrate a release both internally and externally, often simultaneously or with a particular sequential timing.

- Social networks (see the *Appendix* for a list of these) are extremely important but must be carefully managed. Make sure that your Facebook or other social network posting is up-to-date, but here are some guidelines:

  ✓ Treat a social network as you would a professional conversation with a new acquaintance who is an unknown.

  ✓ Be careful of grammar, spelling, wording, and style on what you post. Let others damage their brand image by posting sloppy statements or throwing around outlandish opinions.

- ✓ Do not ever post your entire resume on a social network. Instead, you can indicate carefully chosen tidbits, or things to generate interest.

- ✓ Do not ever indicate that you are unemployed on a social network.

- ✓ Do not ask for a job on a social network.

- ✓ Do state your accomplishments in a generic manner on a social network. Do not mention companies or entities where your have worked or dates. Instead, use the "functional resume" format in which you state things like "successfully introduced several new products for a major consumer goods company" or "led the offshore mineral exploration program for a major resources company" or "developed, taught, and trained instructors in a new course on environmental economics for a major university" or "managed the planning, subcontracting, and building program for a major nationwide housing developer."

- ✓ Do state your education, training, and certification in a generic manner, but do not give anything that might foster identity theft, scams, or surreptitious and unwarranted invasions of your privacy.

- ✓ Include your contact information in a "blind manner" like a specially dedicated email address so as to avoid identity theft and spam.

- ✓ Do not give away career opportunity information on a social network.

- ✓ If you get a response via a social network, proceed cautiously, screening the respondent until you know who you are dealing with. Follow the *Section 2.4* process for building qualified career contacts.

- Eventually, you may want professional public relations help and there might be resources within your company, or through a professional society, in addition to contacting one of the many excellent PR groups that exist.

Additional Career Marketing Plan Elements

You must think of yourself as a product or service that needs to be fully and correctly defined, and must be targeted to meet real needs in the marketplace. So, your *Career Marketing Plan* should start with an accurate definition of your expertise, knowledge, experience, perspective and unique abilities. And then just as in any marketing plan, you must define the market opportunities completely: geographic areas, industry segments, willingness-to-pay (compensation), competition, forecasts, and so forth.

As you go through this *Guide*, it will become clearer that the combination of your *Career Information System*, your *Career Contacts System*, and your *Career Opportunities System* will help you complete your *Career Marketing Plan*. Namely, it is OK to put together a draft version of your *Career Marketing Plan*, initially, but you will not be able to complete the *Marketing Plan* until you have developed all of the other career support systems that are advocated here.

****

2.7 ALWAYS HAVE A PLAN-B AND AN EXIT STRATEGY

Do not permit yourself to become lulled into a false sense of job security in your present position. It is always wise to have a "Plan-B" or contingency plans thought out in case unforeseen changes occur in your position. Here are some suggestions in this regard:

- As best as you can, through the *Contacts* and *Opportunities Systems* previously described, it is helpful to have "ready-to-go" contacts available, if not "soft job offers" on file.

- Through professional certification or licensing, often sponsored and paid for by your present company to keep you up-to-date, you can keep your value in the open market as current as possible.

- Internal to your present company, try to keep a log of backup opportunities within the company – people you know and who have even asked you if you would be interested in joining their organization sometime in the future; growth divisions that are hiring and not shrinking; moving from staff to field and R&D; even taking a downgrade to something that could fit if necessary. Your best "Plan-B" can often be opportunities within your current company.

- Also, try to keep a log of backup opportunities in the same industry, namely, contacts you have already developed and are ready-to-go, so that you could even "call on your cell phone from your boss's office and get a job offer over the phone on the spot." Do you know who is hiring at any moment? Have you cultivated "ready-to-go" situations?

- Strive to have prior written offers kept on file; for which you thanked them but declined and kept in touch very diplomatically, for example via friendly emails and cards.

- Remember that "backup opportunities" can include teaching and training situations, consulting and outsourcing opportunities, and your own business ventures.

- A backup opportunity could also include an overseas assignment in an international division of a domestic entity. This is especially true if you have remained fluent in several languages.

81

- Remain friendly, courteous, and professional if surprised by any sudden employment situation change. Do not let such a change derail your career perspective and career development.

- If you are suddenly asked to take a new assignment, you must have both an immediate reaction thought out for such a situation, plus a longer term plan ready to go. Remember that you might be asked to give an answer on-the-spot. If you give away yourself through choice of words, voice tone, expressions, or body language you might either lose out on a real opportunity or be acquiescing to an undesirable career move. If appropriate, ask to get back to the person making the offer, even if it sounds great immediately. Then think of your options. Sometimes passing up a "supposed opportunity" can keep yourself out of an impossible situation such as working for a person who is known to be a real problem, or being involved in some harebrained venture that has not been thought out but needs "rescuing." If you say "yes with a smile," but then show professional skills in evaluation and screening of the situation before you make a final commitment, then you very likely will come out a winner.

- Have a written draft of a job reference "ready-to-go" if the unknown arises and you have to leave abruptly, and get one or more copies signed by the appropriate person(s). Hand this to managers and try to get them to sign it on the spot. Remember, get references before leaving, not after the fact when people might disappear, or do not want to be bothered, or will write up something totally useless.

- Sometimes companies ask people to "raise their hands" in a meeting after a merger-acquisition, in order to see who might be interested in taking a severance package. They want to get a headcount to determine the cost, or to test who will not be loyal to the acquiring company, or other hidden agendas. Someone at the back of the room might be writing down names.

- Do your own "exit interviews" to thank everyone and say that you want to keep in touch, with both higher-ups and peers and any valuable key players, and get complete contact information. Don't wait for some human resources person to give a short exit session, ask "any questions?" and then take your company badge and escort you to the door. Remain in control of such an exit process.

****

2.8 WHAT TO DO ABOUT OUTSOURCING AND OFFSHORING

At some point in your career, you might encounter the matter of outsourcing of your work to a contractor, often located offshore. Companies do this for many reasons, but perceived cost, accounting factors including overseas tax rates, and focus on their core strategy are the most common motivating factors for outsourcing.

If you do routine tasks on your job, for example if you happen to be a lawyer researching legal databases for prior cases, or another professional doing something primarily on remote databases, your job might be ripe for outsourcing. If you do something which requires a lot of experience, including face-to-face interaction with many individuals, it is unlikely that your job could ever be outsourced or sent offshore. But be aware that outsourcing is moving to a higher level than routine answering of telephone calls, programming, computer help desks, and so forth, and advanced engineering design work, complex computer programming, web design, are all likely to be outsourced.

If you perceive that your position, or even an entire division (you might be in charge of hundreds of people) might be outsourced, then make sure that your "Plan-B" is kept up-to-date and ready-to-go, as discussed in the previous *Section 2.7*. An exit strategy for a position, no matter what level or how involved and critical your work may be, is always an important "insurance factor" in case you encounter an outsourcing situation.

There have been some spectacular failures of outsourcing. For example, in 2002, a major U.S. bank announced a multi-billion outsourcing deal with a major domestic IT services company. A number of displaced bank employees were immediately hired with pay cuts by the domestic outsourcing company, but the jobs of many other bank employees went overseas. Then soon after the 2002 outsourcing announcement, this bank merged with another bank, who incidentally had a bad experience with the same outsourcing company, and the outsourcing deal was put on hold, and then reversed and the IT work was brought back in-house ("backsourcing"). But by that time, many employees had left or been put in very uncertain career positions, and the management structure

84

was fractured. Obviously the original perceived cost-savings of outsourcing were far exceeded by the cost of reversing the decision and the costs of confusion and project disruption.

Another approach to the outsourcing situation is to be proactive and respond with a proposal to the company that you would be glad to do the exact same work as you are doing now, but would form your own contracting entity, and have them outsource to you. The benefit to the company is that you know the work details much better than any new outsource group or offshore group that has to be trained starting from zero. Of course the company wants to save overhead like health benefits and pension payments, and also to do the same work at a much lower cost, and maybe save taxes. But your proposal could take all of this into account, if you do a business plan and a complete business case for them to show the real costs, including a factor for customer aggravation, quality decrease, turnover, training, and changes in market position.

Companies often either have a domestic consulting firm retained to look at outsourcing options, or receive unsolicited proposals from offshore outsourcing firms, as precursors to a final outsourcing decision. You can fight a bad outsourcing decision by raising a host of issues and problems, and cost elements that only an experienced insider like yourself would know about. Do not be afraid to professionally and tactfully warn about such matters -- raising a stink might save your job, and you could come out ahead in the end. If the outsourcing decision turns sour, as many have, you at least have your professional pride, and might even be called back to head the effort to fix the situation.

(Later in this book, you will see in *Section 2.17* a discussion of consulting and contracting as a career path. This discussion is highly relevant for those who encounter an outsourcing or offshoring of their job.)

Finally, a last resort can be to join the outsourcing or offshoring firm itself. Often you might have to take a pay cut to do so, but remember that they will need managers, trainers, and organizers to get the effort off the ground. If you know the work intimately, you have a high value proposition and can either be an independent consultant to them or become part of their staff, even temporarily. Emphasize success for both the outsourcing firm and the company writing the contract.

****

2.9 SURVIVAL STEPS – INTERIM EMPLOYMENT

Changing jobs and reorienting your career takes time. There are many statistics on how long it will take someone to find a new position, from a few weeks to over a year, depending on the industry and their particular level and field of interest. You want to avoid like the plague wasting your valuable time standing in an unemployment line at a job fair or at an open house, when you could be pursuing opportunities on a proactive contact-building basis, often with no competition from other job seekers.

There is tremendous prejudice and illegal discrimination against

unemployed persons. Many companies will not even accept a resume from anyone who admits that they are currently unemployed. A lot of resume screeners and initial interview screeners are told to diligently look for "gaps" in resumes, as if this is some kind of fatal flaw or even fraud. Even if someone states that they took time off to travel or to take advantage of a particular educational opportunity, or to give attention to a newborn or adopted child, they might immediately be eliminated from consideration. These harsh facts are additional reasons why a "resume-only" approach to career planning and job search is very undesirable.

This is also why you should always have a "Plan B" to deal with unpredictable reorganizations, layoffs, force reductions, or acquisitions which might arise and threaten your current career position. This is why you must never be lulled into a false sense of security in your current position. Think in the direction of *prevailing* in the face of unknowns and difficulties, and *excelling* in your career, as you remain totally *in control of your career*, not merely whipped around and de-motivated by events.

A *"Plan B"* should not be one-dimensional, but rather you should make a list of "what if" questions and possible circumstances and then develop answers to each "what if." Of course, this is a time to consult all of your resources, including especially your *Career Contacts System* and your *Career Opportunities System*.

Do NOT think of yourself as "out of a job" but rather having embarked on a new career path, either temporarily or permanently. Do not panic, and remain positive. Do not add to your stress level, and convert your anger to action. Remember all of the motivation and persistence information in *Step 1* of this guide.

Do NOT "take time off" and go on a vacation or just decide to give yourself a good rest and stay at home relaxing. You have much to do and should not waste a moment. You should build momentum immediately.

Do NOT immediately go to the Internet and start sending out resumes to everything you see. This is a waste of time. Avoid such useless busywork. Instead, form your career plans and start your action plans to work real contacts and opportunities.

Give yourself a new job, to protect your career and resume and experience history. Form an entity, start a website, call several friends or associates who have also been laid off and make them business partners. Assess your skills and experience. There are many platforms for starting a free website. If you don't have a PC, go to the library where web access is free. Each of your partners will agree to protect all others, and act as references in the future if needed. If anybody wants to know your client customers, tell them that the clients insist on confidentiality. But you might be surprised and find one or more real paying customers who need your services.

It is easier said than done, but it is ideal to have over a year of savings and investment on which you can rely to tide you over a period between jobs or slumps in self-employment. Getting yourself on a "cash basis" so that you are not carrying a house mortgage, car loans, and credit card payments should also be your goal. In this way, you will feel relieved of the obligation to stay in an undesirable job simply to keep up with your debts. It will give you a new sense of freedom to pursue real career goals and to accomplish things that you really want to do in your life.

If you are now between jobs and in debt, have confidence that you will come through this period in your life and then pursue a career path and goals that will surpass anything you might have accomplished in the past. Let this situation be a motivator to never be in this situation again in your life. Do not forget the pain. Do not let a beneficial amnesia to set in when you recover, such that you fall back into the same false sense of job security, and take on debts over your head.

Remember, your positive focus should be to develop yourself as a very valuable person in the workforce, to publicize and control this fact, and to proactively seek out opportunities. When you put yourself in this context, being between jobs becomes a detail.

Now to the business at hand. It is sometimes necessary to seek interim employment to cover expenses between employment situations. If possible, such interim employment should be related to your career goals and abilities and interests, so here are some suggestions.

- Any interim job should be in some way related to your career plan. If you have been a marketing manager who has been let go, try to find a sales position, or a telemarketing or telephone market research position, especially in an industry where you have had experience. If such an interim position is part-time, it will give you the time needed to continue your career-focused job search, using the *Career Information, Career Contacts,* and *Career Opportunities Systems* and databases as described in *Sections 2.3, 2.4,* and *2.5.*

- If you know how to handle yourself on the phone, and have marketing or sales experience, you can do market research on one or more subjects, then analyze the results, formulate the results, write a report, and sell the report, and write articles on the findings. This will take a high degree of initiative, and not all of us are cut out to take on such a venture. Be aware of the consumer "do not call list" laws.

- If you have been involved in IT, networking, or web services and have been laid off, then consider help-desk, computer programming, or network technician interim employment. You also might find a part-time teaching position at a local technical institute, a community college or a university, for a subject related to your previous employment and career focus. You can also merely hang tear-off adds on bulletin boards in stores for PC debugging and repair, or PC virus and malware removal, or cell phone servicing -- all in accordance with your own level of experience.

- If you are a licensed and experienced carpenter, electrician, or plumber who is between jobs because of a housing slump, you can of course seek situations for home or commercial servicing, either via unobtrusive local ads or by contacting the building managers of local or regional office buildings. And you can contact technical training institutes for part-time teaching situations.

- If you have obtained a CDL (Commercial Drivers License) as a backup insurance for unforeseen employment breaks, then you will find that there is a constant demand for drivers of trucks, buses, and commercial vehicles. These can be either full-time or part-time.

- Sometimes, one can take a quick course on something that is in great demand, and turn this into an interim employment opportunity. But be careful not to learn something only to find out that the job market is flooded with people who have the same skill and training, but with more experience than you have.

- Often we have hobbies that can lead directly to interim employment opportunities. If you garden as a hobby, and know plants and landscaping, you can offer your services, even off-season, to help homeowners and even commercial property managers improve their gardens and landscaping. If you fish or hunt, you can contact retail stores who need someone knowledgeable to assist customers. If you repair your own car, you can contact auto servicing establishments (although they might expect you to be licensed or certified).   If you play a musical instrument, you can teach part-time locally.

- A last-gasp is often working a retail counter or pumping gas. But often these situations can be part-time, leaving you with a schedule for pursuing career opportunities through the *Systems* described in this *Career Control Guide*.

Lastly, at all costs, remember to protect you greatest assets – your self-esteem, motivation and persistence. Do not let yourself fall into depression over being between jobs, or lapse into a state of inaction. Remember that you are unique in this world, and have much to contribute.

****

2.10 SECURITY AND CAREER PLANNING

In today's online, mobile, and electronic information environment, everything we do is subject to security concerns. There are hackers just trying to cause trouble because of their emotional and mental dysfunction, or criminal hackers trying to steal information, money, or identities. There are information terrorists trying to disrupt activities of businesses, governments, or individuals because of disturbed ideologies or psychotic dissatisfactions. And in the career environment, there are those who are competing for jobs and cannot make it on their own and want to rob you of information and even disrupt your career planning and development.

In addition, there can be many security concerns related to your career within your existing company or employment situation. If you are a carpenter, electrician, plumber, painter, or mason who works on new home developments or home improvement contracts, be careful what you say to your fellow workers about opportunities that you have heard of elsewhere or even just rumors. The information might help someone beat you to the next opportunity. The same within the walls of a company. If anyone knows that you are looking around the industry for a better position, they could deliberately or inadvertently spill the beans in their conversations with others, and cause you problems, including the loss of a job the next time there is a round of cost-cutting.

Be aware of constant and pervasive surveillance, for real or imagined security reasons, or just because of a paranoid attitude of snooping, voyeurism, and control within a company. Today, bathrooms, elevators, hallways, offices, meeting rooms, doorways, walkways, and parking lots have security cameras. Sometimes also microphones are placed strategically to monitor conversations. Of course, email messaging, voicemail, live phone conversations, mobile text messaging, Internet access by sites visited and downloads, are all part of this pervasive surveillance and invasion of privacy.

You must use only a home computer for career-related communications. Even then, you will want to often use pseudonyms and a multitude of carefully coded email addresses. Everything you send will reveal the IP address of your home PC. Some of your messaging should be encrypted, but of course if you correspond via email with a career information source or contact, it will have to be unencrypted until you establish a relationship. If your own end of a communication link is secure but the receiving end is not, then there is no security at all.

Educate yourself on all of the security concerns and tricks on the Internet and on mobile communications. Make sure that you have a personal firewall at your home PC or on a mobile laptop. Activate virus and malware detection software and keep it up to date with a subscription to an automatic updating service. Update any passwords and online IDs frequently, and keep a database of these IDs and passwords on a backup disk or disks. Never enter any demographic information at an opt-in site that is not secure (https, and padlock icon in the PC "tray").

Finally, be smart and cautious about all of your career information, including sources, contacts, and opportunities. Keep most of this on backup disks, password protected, and in many cases encrypted. You will be grateful for your efforts if you never experience a personal information or communications security breach. All you need is one fatal incident to derail your career development and control, and disrupt many years of effort.

Here are some additional security points to keep in mind.

✓   Sometimes company HR groups or retained search firms post fake jobs on the Internet to find out who in the company is "looking" and what they are revealing about themselves. Of course, companies need to keep intellectual property secure, including what is in the minds of their key employees. In fact, some companies have actually sued employees who have changed jobs and gone to a competitor, trying to block them from working, and claiming that a non-compete agreement might be violated, even without any documented incidents.

✓   Postings on social networking sites, or comments on a blog site, or any other online information that you create must be treated with extreme caution. A blog comment posted anonymously or with a pseudonym still might be traced to your originating IP address.

✓   Walking around a trade show or a job fair and freely handing out copies of your resume is a gigantic mistake. The same is true about posting your resume online on as many sites as you can. Your purpose must be to identify and filter the real career contacts and career opportunities, and to tightly control who knows anything about yourself and when. You will lose control of your career by such actions, you may find that the effect is permanent and irreparable. The potential for misinterpretation and abuse is great, and information that goes out-of-date quickly can cause you to be badly positioned.

✓   Lastly, when you have filtered and evaluated real career contacts and opportunities, you can gradually disclose information relevant to the opportunity, and withhold anything that might damage the contact or opportunity. Remain in control of your career.

****

2.11 PUBLISHING YOUR WAY TO A GREAT CAREER

For centuries, publishing has been a time-proven way to establish one's self as an expert on a subject, to display abilities and knowledge, to advocate ideas and ideologies, and to gain the respect of others. Benjamin Franklin published himself the *"Poor Richard's AlmanacK"* as a subscription and not only earned a lot of money, but developed a base of readers, and established a reputation for himself in colonial America.

Publishing puts you in control. Of course editors have to make your submission fit their particular publication, and like to correct and add their own ideas -- but you are the author and are in control to negotiate the suggested changes, and even to walk away and go to another publisher. You can also publish your work on your own. Walt Whitman published *"Leaves of Grass"* himself, most likely because he did not want any editors messing with his work.

A few guidelines. If you are currently working in an organization, it is important for you to follow their rules for publishing. When you hired on, you may have signed various Agreements regarding intellectual property and publishing. Review any such items. Then find out discretely through your HR and Legal departments what their rules are. If nothing has ever been documented, don't assume that there are no rules or restrictions. It is understood that an employee should never have a conflict of interest, and must resolve any such conflict in a satisfactory manner. Employees of course cannot give away internal information that will aid competitors. Employees cannot open up issues outside of the organization that will potentially damage markets, financial analysis, and governmental oversight. Don't start by asking your immediate boss -- even if he or she is very supportive. And also be aware that publishing opens new questions and issues. Many bosses feel threatened by an employee who is more knowledgeable than they are, or has more visibility within and outside of the organization. And of course, control-freak management might really react negatively, and try to stop you from "giving away company secrets" or other excuses. But if your boss has published a number of articles and perhaps books, then you have a great opening for a discussion of your own potential publication. Also, if you have published before both within and outside of the organization, then this will help greatly. Lastly, most organizations have some kind of in-house publication, and this will be a "safe" place to start. Even if there is no such internal publication, you can make suggestions on the value to the company of starting one, and can

94

simply suggest an internal "white paper" on a subject, and circulate discretely a "draft" - with follow-up versions of the draft and welcome comments and suggestions. However, watch out for some others overtly or secretly stealing your own ideas.

If conflicts arise within your organization you have many alternatives. But remain calm, positive, and avoid confrontations. You can publish an article without any identification of your current organization, but published under your name. You can even create a pseudonym, but this is not recommended and will not help you develop an industry position and reputation. If you face a dragged-out stalling internally do not let it get to you. Send reminders that there are publishing deadlines. Advocate the benefit to the company in the marketplace if they have increased visibility through your publication.

Publication Options

There are many different ways that you can publish something today. It is a different world from many years ago when authors would type up a manuscript and mail it out to one or more publishers, and then wait for acceptance or rejection letters to come. Here are several of the many choices that you have:

1) **Paper book traditional publication**: You can of course write an entire book and submit it to a publisher. Go to the websites of various book publishers and gather information and/or call them and ask about book submittal procedures. Look at what other books they are currently selling. Go to a physical bookstore and look at the books of various publishers. You must be prepared, that if you are a first-time author, that they will be somewhat skeptical that you will actually finish a book, and that it will be truly viable in the marketplace. Therefore, you need to sell yourself and also the need for such a topic, and your special approach. If you have much experience, and have a lot of contacts, they will be much more interested. Publishers often have book guidelines for authors, and you can look at these guidelines online or via a download, or request a paper document. Often, all that is needed is a "Proposal" for a book -- consisting of a table of contents, and an initial chapter, and perhaps other information on yourself and the topic and the market for such a book. For a first-time author, they will

seldom offer you an advance. Once you get started on a book, they will usually want you to sign a contract, with many terms and conditions, including giving them exclusive rights to publish other books that you might write, and even requiring you to follow up this initial book with other books, over a defined period of time. The advantage of dealing with an established publisher is their ability to edit, print, and distribute books. This relieves you of much overhead. However, they will make most of the profit, and pay you merely an author's royalty for books that are sold.

2) ***Paper book self-publishing:*** If you think that you can orchestrate the many tasks needed to write, publish, distribute, and market a new paper book, then you need to set up a complete schedule, even a business plan, for all that is needed. The advantage is that you will be making a much greater profit than going through a publishing house. However. you will be trading a lot of your own time for this potential profit. And you might or might not do a better marketing job. The ball is in your court.

3) ***Electronic publishing:*** The electronic book market is now exploding, because of the growth of the Internet and mobile devices, and also because of new e-reader devices. Amazon now sells more e-books for their Kindle e-reader than they do paper books. Electronic publishing has made it somewhat easier to be a self-publisher, but many of the fundamentals of authoring and publishing remain unchanged.

4) ***Electronic or paper articles:*** Instead of trying to write an entire book you can write an article, either long and comprehensive, or short and in a commentary style. You can also post "white papers" on your own Facebook page or your own personal website or blog, and can enter comments on many forums and websites. You can offer reviews of books that you have read and have them listed on Amazon or other high-traffic sites. All of the above electronic online publications can be mentioned to organizations and individuals with whom you wish to be associated, for career development and job opportunities. But be organized, keep close track of what you put online, and make sure that whatever you publish adds to your background and does not detract. Be objective, and opportunity-oriented as far as industry developments and trends.

Determine Where to Publish and What is Currently Out There

You need to look over many publications in your field and see what is being written, and also what the requirements are for submitting articles. There will be "authors guidelines" listed on both websites and on an identification page of each magazine, journal, or periodical. Check out the "style" of each publication, and also the organizational level and industry reputation of authors of various articles. Some publications include only articles written by their staff, and some of these internally-written items are not "signed" by the author. You want to avoid these, because they will not help you develop an industry reputation. You might want to start by offering commentaries on articles, that can appear in a "Letters to the Editor" section of the publication, and then build on these as references when you submit an actual article.

Once you start publishing, you will gain momentum and develop your own procedures and style. But be careful to safeguard your industry position and reputation.

How to Write an Article in 10 Steps

Writing non-fiction is not something you do out of pure "inspiration" or as "stream-of-consciousness." Rather, you need to plan what you will do, get information together, and often edit and re-write many times. You need to fit the goal precisely.

Here are *"Ten-Steps-to-Publication"* that will help you in developing publications that will help your career development.

1) Publication Analysis

You must first familiarize yourself with all of the print and online opportunities for your publishing. What kind or articles are typically included in each magazine, journal, newspaper, or online site that you have identified? What is their circulation and who do you think they are targeting? What is their style – upbeat, practical, how-to, funny, skeptical, and so forth?

Next, you need to identify their publication guidelines. Look for the name of the editor and their contact information. Do they mainly have articles written by their staff, or are most of their articles submitted by outside authors? Often they will have a "publications guidelines" document which they can mail or email or you can download.

You should create a list or database of publications relevant to your career interests, with all contact information, guidelines, and some notes about how important you think each publication is to your career development.

2)   *Published Article Theme(s)*

What should you write about? This is a key question, and can shape your career development, in both positive and negative ways. For example, a practical, prosaic article positions you as a no-nonsense person who can get the job done. A proposal type of article positions you as an innovative person, who might have insights into new business opportunities. An extremely detailed article positions you as a specialist who could be of high value for a particular area. A general article positions you as a person with a good view of the field, but no particular specialty. Of course, you can publish many articles in a field, which vary in both theme and style, but you will want to maintain a degree of consistency in your "publishing persona" and the relationship to your overall *Career Public Relations System.*

You need to build a relationship with publication editors, proving that you can write well on topics important to the field, and which fit in with both the style and themes of the publication. Also, the length of the article needs to comply with what they are accustomed to fit in with their general layout, although sometimes publications will feature a series of articles in successive parts in order to accommodate an important subject.

You can "brainstorm" themes for articles and keep a list. After reading print and online items, jot down your thoughts and ideas, some of which could lead to your own articles on a related or entirely new subject. Go through your *Career Information System* and identify current and related and innovative themes. Through interaction (live, email, etc.) with those in your *Career Contacts System*, you might also touch on matters leading to themes for articles. However you do this identification of themes, keep it all very organized, and try not to lose track of even small details which could lead to important articles in the future. You don't want to have regrets that you had identified a theme for an article but did not follow up, and then see in print someone else's article on the same theme.

Lastly, maintain security on the themes which you identify, and do not give away anything to those who compete with your career goals or who could damage your career development. In your present career position, either at a company or in your own business, you never want to publish something that gives away a new business opportunity, nor reveals any intellectual property, or violates a non-compete agreement. Once you publish, in many cases your information is "in the public domain" and can be leveraged by anyone.

3)   *Published Article Title*

The title of an article does several things at once. It attracts the attention of readers, it helps editors compose an edition, it tells the reader what to expect in the article, and may even setup for a discussion and controversy. So choose a title appropriate to the situation and the intended audience. Make a list of "brainstormed titles" and then narrow down the list. Sometimes, you can use a main title to attract attention, and then a sub-title to add a plain-vanilla description of the material.

(4) *Published Article Handles*

A good way to get started on an article is to list what authors often call "handles" for their writing. "Handles" can be anything that comes to mind, but are mostly key points to be made in the publication. Namely, things that you MUST cover, even giving examples. But also, Handles could often be some cogent occurrences or events that will add the right flavor and emphasis. Be comprehensive in making a list of Handles. Brainstorm ideas, and research to see what is happening on the topic. Include competitive activities, markets and products, regulation, scams and security, global activities - in order words, be comprehensive up-front.

(5) Published Article Research and Competitive Analysis

From your *Career Information System*, you should be keeping in touch with what is happening and this can be a great resource for background material when authoring a new publication. But, you need to dig deeper to really write something that is relevant and fully aware of current activities regarding a particular topic. If you are writing something which is mostly "historical" in nature, then make sure that you research all of the previous important publications on the subject. Skipping something major will be recognized by readers as a major error. You can also derive a new point-of-view by looking backwards with insights that the authors did not or even could not have in previous writings. If you are adopting a "contrarian" view about how things are being done, then it is important to know how the present thoughts and attitudes were originally formulated.

If you are writing about the current state of a particular subject, then you must make sure that you keep up with the pace of change. Leaving out something new that changes your whole perspective can be a fatal error. Sometimes authors or editors insert the term "at the time of this writing" as a caveat, but this might weaken the writing and cause some readers to skip ahead to another page.

Every author develops their favorite sources for material and their own style for researching efficiently, and you should work on adopting a very efficient research process for yourself. But be careful to not get caught up in a single mindset that is trapped by going back to the same old sources. It is useful to look for other global sources, different segments, and non-traditional sources. But beware of unsubstantiated hearsay, and the deliberately iconoclastic perspectives that one sees on Internet blogs. Just like a good news reporter, you need multiple sources that confirm one another before you accept any research material.

Lastly, you must be highly organized in sourcing your research material, keeping track of references precisely, and deciding if you want to use an exact referenced quotation. Adhere to the highest standards of giving credit to sources, out or respect for other authors and respect for your readers, and in compliance with laws about plagiarism and misrepresentation.

(6) Sections for Your Publication

Now you have to break the handles and research material into "baskets" of items that relate to one another, and will become sections of your publication. Your can have several types of flows among the sections in a publication. Sometimes authors will write a short piece that starts with initial statements that "put a stake in the ground." Then they will continue the article in support of the initial statements, or even break down and defeat the initial statements. Alternatively, authors can construct an article in the "garden path" mode, building one section and statement after another, and leading to the final conclusion, almost like a mystery novel, with even a surprise ending. In a "garden path" publication, different opposing perspectives and facts can be included along the way, leaving the reader to wonder what will win out and what the author will finally conclude. And lastly, writing on a topic that is fast-developing will often avoid any firm conclusions, but hopefully will avoid trite statements like "time will tell" and "stay tuned for the conclusion."

(7) Style of Your Publication

Many authors eventually adopt a particular signature style. However, always remember that what you write must fit the particular situation – including the reading audience, the editor's prerogatives, the publication's particular slant, and the "here-and-now" setting. And an author's particular style often evolves over time during his or her career.

Remember that what you write is a permanent record and cannot be retracted. It will be a major element in defining who you are, what you know, what you can do, your professional persona, your perspectives, and how you view opportunities. If you want to be one who is out in front in your field, then you will often want to focus in any publication on where things are going. If you want to focus on the nuts-and-bolts of things in a field, then you will want to keep away from anything that might be speculative. And if you want to emphasize opportunities, you will want to keep away from merely solving operational problems that inevitable arise.

Whatever style you adopt, make sure that your writing is clear and concise. Being excessively wordy will distract readers, and will ingratiate you with editors and block your chances of getting in print. Make things easy for editors.

(8) Draft Your Publication

After following the above 7 steps, you will be in a great position to start writing. But don't try a draft until you are totally ready and have followed the above steps - otherwise you will waste a lot of time in starting a draft and leaving it unfinished only to go back to things that you should have done in preparation for an actual first draft.

Don't dwell on perfection when completing an initial draft. If you create some cute wording that you like initially, so much the better. But remember that at this point you will have to come back for proof-reading and re-wording and fixing, at least several times. Just move on and get something down, covering all of the "handles" that you initially identified.

(9) Review and Edit

Once you finish an initial draft, you need to rewrite, reword, and correct. A few tips in doing this. First, run a spell-check on the word-processor file. Then read through and correct grammar, and shorten and tighten the text. Then read through from the beginning, critiquing the flow, the message, and the content from a reader's and editor's point-of-view.

(10) Publication Submittal

Now that you have completed the above steps, it is time to send your proposed article off to the targeted publication, usually to the editor. Work with them for any revisions that are needed to fit the article an upcoming issue. You then have made a statement to the world -- make sure that this is the message that you want to send out.

****

2.12 WEB PRESENCE DECISIONS

The public Internet, via the World Wide Web, is now the world's undisputed global information network. Furthermore, the Mobile Web is revolutionizing both business and personal communications, and the mobile smartphone and tablet devices are rapidly becoming data processing platforms of choice. In addition "cloud computing," namely web-based computing, is taking a share of the traditional mainframe-based and PC-based business computing market. And lastly, social networking websites are becoming major portals and platforms for communicating personal information in a non-real-time mode.

How does all of the above affect your career planning and development? The answer depends on the industry sector, among many other factors, but as we look to the future, an online web presence will affect virtually all career-related activities. Therefore, use of the Web and your presence on the Web are mandatory elements in your overall career management and control.

The first important principle to which you should steadfastly adhere is this:

"Do not post or enter any information on a website that might hurt your career or in any way relinquish control of your career to others."

What does this mean? It means that:

- You need to control the Web, and make sure that the Web does not control you.

- You should not post your resume online.

- You should not post your resume on a social networking website.

- Instead, you should remain in control of your life and career by carefully selecting *who* should know anything about yourself, *what* they should know, and *when* they should know anything.

- You should leverage the power of the Web to publicize yourself in a well-managed and controlled manner.

- You should use the Web to feed your *Career Information System*, your *Career Contacts System*, and your *Career Opportunities System*.

- You should also use the Web to keep your *Career Roadmap* up to date, including all of the eight basic *Roadmap* elements described in *Section 1.6*.

****

2.13 SPEAKING YOUR WAY TO A GREAT CAREER

There are conferences, conventions, and trade fairs for virtually every business area that you can name. These events are an important way to set yourself apart from the pack and gain control of your career through public speaking. Many trade associations have regional and local chapters, and you could speak less formally at such smaller meetings.

Some of you might detest speaking in public and be saying – "Oh No" -- and others who enjoy such speaking opportunities and might have done this before are saying – yes, you're right. If you do not enjoy speaking in public, you have two choices: Either start a program to make yourself into an effective speaker, or just don't do it -- you have other choices such as publishing in print or online.

However, internal to an organization, and in front of customers and third parties, it is hard to develop a career without being an effective speaker. So if you need improvement, take a course, join Toastmasters, and get some books on becoming an effective speaker. Also, you should make sure that the presentation materials that you use are of the highest caliber. Learn how to use PowerPoint and a PC Projector with a remote control, so that your presentations will be powerful and highly effective. Even if you are meeting internally with one or two persons, if you are covering a complete topic that might take more than 15 minutes, it is OK to set up an electronic slide presentation -- just don't overdue formalities and keep it appropriate and flexible for the particular situation.

How to Give a Talk

- Relax – always talk as if in a small group. This way everyone in the audience will feel that you are speaking to them directly and understanding their own individual situation, even if you need to generalize for the entire audience.

- Introduce yourself, even if there is a formal pre-speaker introduction by a conference session coordinator.

- Don't talk down, but explain everything. Avoid undefined terminology, undefined abbreviations, and undefined acronyms. Of course, when speaking to only a few people who all are familiar with a topic or project, you don't need to overdo the business of undefined acronyms. And use the "lingo of the trade" as appropriate.

- When you are in the public domain – share openly. But safeguard proprietary information, trade secrets, proprietary market information, protected financial numbers, any advance product information, and anything that competitors would find useful.

- Be accessible – if people come up after your talk and want your business card, be ready to follow up.

- Pace your presentation carefully and keep on schedule. Don't run over your allotted time, and leave time for questions. Don't let one disruptive individual shout out a question and hold up the talk unfairly for the whole audience.

- Know the audience – who are they, what do they know, and what do they want to know and learn.

- Be prepared to give out copies of everything. If something should not be handed out, leave it out of your presentation.

- Introduce every slide before opening it. But don't just say "on the next slide" again and again. Instead, tell them what to expect before you bring it up.

- Follow the time-proven "preacher format." Namely, tell them what you're going to tell them, then tell them, then tell them what you told them.

- Make sure that there is a logical flow through the presentation.

- Talk between lines on a slide, and paraphrase as appropriate – don't read a slide, but add additional useful information and even anecdotes to add interest and show the depth of your knowledge.

- Have excellent materials, but don't make any one slide too complicated that it will chew up a lot of time. A slide should take two minutes or less. Mix media as appropriate, including text, images, video, and even online real-time links. But do not overdo multimedia to the point of distraction. Remember that you and your voice are in control at all times.

- Always use electronic slides and a remote control unit so that you can have instant control of slides and keep eye contact with the audience.

- Your words are important, so choose them carefully.

- Rehearse, rehearse, and rehearse until you could do the whole thing from memory and can visualize every slide in order.

- Dress accordingly, and have a stage presence. Start off with a little humor if appropriate, and a brief anecdote that is relevant. To warm up the audience, congratulate them on being interested in the topic that you will cover, since this is a very important topic, related to key opportunities.

- End with a thank you.

****

2.14 CERTIFICATION AND LICENSING TO AFFIRM YOUR KNOWLEDGE AND EXPERTISE

An important step in furthering your career is through professional certification. This is especially important in a number of technical areas, but can apply to almost any area. If you have never looked into certification opportunities, start with going to the website: http://en.wikipedia.org/wiki/Professionalcertification . There you will find many, but certainly not all, of the professional certification opportunities for many fields.

What does certification do for you? It is a way to bypass any experience gaps in your resume, and also to show that you can do the job. You can also look at certification as merely a personal thing -- to prove to yourself that you are up-to-date in an area, even test your own skill level. But guard against becoming a "certification junkie" -- namely collecting certification names and acronyms just for the sake of it, and to the detriment of broader professional development.

If you work at a company where most of the staff have earned their certification in a particular area, then it is mandatory for you to acquire one or more appropriate certifications. For example, in a civil engineering firm, most everyone will have a P.E. (Professional Engineer) certification, which is often required in various jurisdictions in order to meet regulations. MDs who have certifications beyond formal licensed specialties can not only attract patients, but also earn an increased recognition within the medical profession. The same is true of actuaries, accountants, lawyers, computer programmers, electricians, carpenters, plumbers, auto mechanics, nurses, medical technicians, web designers, language translators, counselors, physical trainers, physical therapists, chiropractors, real estate agents and brokers, project managers, quality assurance specialists, and many other professional career areas.

Of course state-level licensing is required by law for those who practice in the public domain. But there are "training," "tutoring," "advisory," and "coaching" situations which bypass formal licensing. It is advised for the reader to check carefully with local, county, state, and federal regulations for any professional area.

Lastly, a note about the many "quickie" certifications that you may come upon. Evaluate these carefully. Some are merely close to a scam to get you to pay for a session, and then "achieve" a "little

109

certificate" which is totally worthless as an element in your career development. Your time is better spent on achieving a respected certification or licensing, or pursuing a more formal educational program.

****

2.15 YOUR CONTINUING EDUCATION PROGRAM

An important element of your *Career Roadmap* is to enhance your education. Do not delude yourself to believe that you studied everything that you need to know years ago, and that this information will never go out of date. Things can change rapidly and new concepts, products, services, developments, and opportunities are continually arising.

An easy way to add to your formal education is through online degree or non-degree programs. You can also seek grants to make the financial burden easier. But make sure that you study something that will fit your career goals, and actually lead you to better opportunities. The *Appendix* lists several useful online sources, but you can easily find your own sources.

The online options are vast. Here are some examples, and you should creatively research your own educational options on a continuing basis.

- MIT makes over 2000 of their courses available free online through their "Open courseware" program at http://ocw.mit.edu/index.htm, but to actually get course credit toward a degree, you must go through the enrollment process.

- Yale University also makes many courses free online at http://oyc.yale.edu/ through their "Open Yale Courses" program.

- At http://www.openculture.com/freeonlinecourses your can choose among over 350 online free courses from major universities.

- And of course you can search the web for many other online courses that are *free*.

- You can enroll in an online degree program or certificate program for which you have to formally enroll and pay tuition fees, and will earn an actual degree. Originally these types of courses were in the same category as the old "mail-order degree" programs, but today they are much more respectable. Some examples are found at http://www.onlinedegreeprograms.com/ Of course the

111

advantage of a degree-granting or certificate program, as opposed to an entirely free course or program, is that you have a piece of paper to substantiate and certify your educational achievement, and therefore add a concrete element to your career development and value in the career marketplace.

You can of course enroll in a local university degree program, a local county-level community college, or a local adult school. You can in many cases have your current employer pay for and reimburse you for some or all of the local program or individual courses. And in some companies, you can apply for a totally underwritten executive program for an MBA or JD or other degrees, covering all costs including out-of state room, board and tuition.

Before leaving this subject of educational enhancement to your career development, here are a few things to keep in mind when putting the educational component in perspective.

- In some fields, for example the academic or medical worlds, accumulation of degrees and certifications can have high career value. But in some others, for example like pure sales, having an MBA in marketing does not guarantee success at all, but of course might enable one to migrate from sales to sales management or market management.

- When evaluating any course or program, inquire whether there is any practical or hands-on component, if applicable. Sometimes there are co-op programs where course work is closely linked to on-the-job or intern experiences.

- Be constructively skeptical about career education. Will it be worth the time and cost? Will it add to your value in the career marketplace? Be on the lookout for scams where you receive training that is of no value because there are no related jobs.

- If you think that you are highly motivated and organized, consider self-learning the same material, and thoroughly reading and understanding the same textbooks that are used in a program. The previous *Section 2.14* covered Certification and Licensing, and if you have the discipline, you need not take any formal course to prepare for a certification test. But don't kid yourself either. A structured program forces you to follow a fixed schedule

112

and to learn and understand a subject, and some "boot camp" programs include repeats of the training until you finally pass the certification exam.

- Another thing to consider is the tradeoffs between generalized educational programs and more highly specialized programs. Whereas a generalized program based on fundamentals purports to be "futureproof" remember that changes occur in any field. Specialized programs might eventually become obsolete in the career marketplace, but if properly structured, will prepare you for here-and-now career situations and increase you immediate near-term value in the career marketplace.

- A "marquee degree" from a prestige institution can open doors for you in several ways. You will make contacts with other students who presently have or will achieve key positions. You will be at an institution that attracts recruiters from key companies who often will have intern or upper-management development programs open to you. And you will also be adding prestige to your biography and this will help you in publications and in speaking opportunities.

- Educational achievements can increase your motivation and self-esteem, and this fact alone will enhance your career development.

- If you are changing fields, or have limited experience in an area, remember that education and training, coupled with certification, can make up somewhat for a lack of experience. Who would you rather hire -- someone who is well trained and smart but does not have much experience, or someone who has years of experience and accomplishment, but whose education and training occurred years ago and whose knowledge might be out-of-date?

****

2.16 TRADE AND SOCIETY MEMBERSHIPS

It is enriching for you to hear the experiences of others in your industry or profession, and membership in a trade society is a useful way to keep in touch. If appropriate, you can also demonstrate leadership apart from your current position, by being involved in chairing a committee or a study group on an important issue.

If you represent you company on a key committee, you increase your value to your company, but remember that there are dangers. If a trade society adopts something unfavorable to your company, you might be blamed for the result, and your effectiveness might be questioned. But if the society adopts something favorable to your company, you could be a hero.

Membership in trade groups and professional societies has value in a bio, but if you just join and don't leverage the opportunity to develop contacts and to increase your knowledge base, you are wasting your time and money. You must keep a balance in this regard.

If you are a student or just starting out on a new career, you should seriously consider being involved in the activities of a professional society. For students, there is often a reduced membership fee, and the association activities can help you decide on career paths, and develop contacts early in your career.

****

2.17 THE CONTRACTING AND OUTSOURCING CAREER PATHS

Today, the traditional, vertically integrated company that does everything in-house is a thing of the past. Not only are many functions outsourced and subcontracted, but some of the staff sitting in-house can actually be contractors. The advantage for the company is that their fixed overhead can be very small, and that they can readily adjust staff and expenses according to the business cycle, especially if they are involved in highly cyclical market segments.

From the point-of-view of contractors, one might conclude that they are less secure than the permanent employees of an organization. This is not necessarily so. If they are highly skilled in a particular area, their contracting agency will often have a backlog of openings pending, and will want to sign them up for the next situation even before their current assignment ends.

Note that most contract employees must work for an organization through a particular contracting entity. It is rare when a company will contract directly with one particular individual, since special legal agreements must be executed. The alternative is for an individual to incorporate, then call themselves a particular DBA (Doing Business As) name like "J.Jones & Assoc, LLC" and sometimes a company will then contract with that moniker.

What is the advantage of contracting? Firstly, you can often get your foot in the door faster and more easily than being hired as an employee. Secondly, you can charge a lot more than they would pay you as salary. Your could bill $200 per hour or $1000+ per day, and they would feel happy to bring you on and test out your expertise and fit with the company culture. From the contracting company's point-of-view, contacting is an expense, and they usually will budget for each department an annual amount for consultants and contractors, whereas to hire someone they need headcount approval and this might require a much more complicated process. When companies impose a "hiring freeze" they often then just turn around and increase their expenses for consultants and contractors, in order to meet the needs of the business. You can use this to your advantage.

Often people are brought into a company as contractors, and if the opportunity grows, and the contracting situation is favorable to the company, the contracted-for individual is offered a permanent employee position, at a reduced rate, but with benefits like health care and pension. Then the individual must decide whether they

115

should hold out for an extension or renegotiation of their contract, to take the permanent position, or to move to another company as a contractor. Keep in mind that many companies will be mindful of security and will attempt to place strict non-compete and non-disclosure constraints on contractors.

You can utilize the same *Career Information System*, *Career Contacts System*, and *Career Opportunities System* that you have already developed for salaried opportunities, to help find consulting and contracting opportunities. Go to Google.com or Yahoo.com or Bing.com or any other search engine, and enter "contract jobs" and you will find links to many sources of contract opportunities. But remember, you need to bring something to the table in terms of skills and opportunities for the company. If you come in as a "heads-down" contractor, the opportunity will be short-term and subject to offshoring.

****

2.18 CONTROL YOUR LIFE THROUGH YOUR OWN BUSINESS VENTURES

Much of the prior material in this *Prevail, Excel: Career Control Guide* has been oriented toward the person working in a particular company, governmental organization, or a particular institution. But do not let this emphasis distract you from your real goal in life – namely a successful career that is paramount for a successful life.

Some of the most rewarding and lucrative opportunities in this world derive from having your own business. This can include a variety of business models. Like direct ownership, or partnering with other persons or business entities, or licensing or taking a share in a prospective innovation through a venture capital entity.

Not everybody is amenable and fit for a personal venture opportunity, and that is OK. However, getting beyond any initial fright-factors can lead to a very rewarding experience. Some envision that running their own business will "set them free," and you are of course in control, but you still have to successfully interact with many others – namely, customers, suppliers and vendors, partners, subcontractors, legal and accounting advisors, and maybe even regulatory, legislative, and other governmental figures. And although you might employ many persons with specialized skills, and might outsource certain functions, you will often find that in order to run and control your business that you have to know something about every single functional and operational aspect. It is unwise to turn everything over to a hired manager who knows more than you know, including what he or she decides to keep secret to himself or herself.

If you own and operate a business, you must be prepared for round-the-clock involvement if necessary. You will never "leave the office" -- the office is you, and it is always with you. Therefore, time-management for a business owner-operator is paramount. And you must be extremely organized.

The form of a business entity can vary from simple to very complex. At one time, the completely "vertically integrated" company tried to do everything themselves. They bought raw materials and made everything they needed. They even shipped things to customers in their own trucks with their own employees. They tried to subcontract nothing. But soon many businesses realized that they could find others who could do certain things better than they themselves could do, and also at less cost.

Today there are businesses that start out with little more than an idea or a license and legal rights to a concept. They subcontract out and outsource virtually everything to make the product or service happen. Then when they have gotten started and have grown successfully, they consider bringing in certain functions and operations under a central entity that they alone control.

Some persons desiring their own business will consider a *franchise*, in order to take advantage of the support and years of experience associated with existing franchises. (See the *Appendix* for resources related to franchises and franchising.) The tradeoff is that a successful franchise location will require a substantial initial investment up front to buy into the franchise. Opening a new location as part of an existing successful franchise will have a very high rate of success for the owner. Existing franchises might have saturated an area, but a reputable franchise will not let someone open a new location that will reduce the revenue and business volume of existing franchisees and leave everyone with a margin squeeze. A totally new franchise that is starting up will require less initial investment, but there will be much higher risk because the market for the product or service is not proven yet, and merely based on market research.

Another alternative is to buy an existing business. You can find out about businesses that are for sale (usually small ones under $20M annual volume), through many sources, including online sites (see the *Appendix* resources), or via print advertising either locally or out-of-town, or sometimes merely through hearsay. Often it is better to approach a small business owner through an intermediary, rather than just direct contact yourself, in order to determine the disposition and condition of the business before making contact and possibly spoiling the opportunity. But eventually, a person-to-person relationship between the seller and buyer needs to be established in order to make for a successful start for the new business owner. The previous owner will have many hidden "secrets" and often financial statements that you will want to know about, and the best way to learn about these is by gaining the confidence of the current owner. If the two parties don't hit it off initially, even if the sale seems to end up with viable terms and conditions, the new owner might find out too late after the fact that he or she was duped.

Business brokers are intermediaries who, just like real estate agents, take a fee for bringing together a seller and a buyer. But of course, these business brokers should have information provided by the seller that tells you a lot about the business for sale. Things like financial statements, assets, markets and customer accounts, key employees, union agreements, geographic trade area including possible global operations, and so forth. Brokers often specialize in a particular business area or industry, such as bottling, food processing, manufacturing, or particular professional services like law firms, accounting firms, and medical practices. Their value-added must be carefully evaluated, and remember that they are working for the seller, and will try to represent the business for sale in the best possible light, and gloss over problems.

Many dream of buying a business with "hidden value" or a business which needs just a "turn-around" in order to be successful. Sometimes this is true, and sometimes it is just wishful thinking on the part of the acquiring party. For example, we sometimes see the same restaurant location turn over every five years, with a new owner-manager coming along, but then finally someone buys the restaurant and makes it into a long-term viable operation. "Hidden value" can be found because of many factors. For example:

- Sometimes new investment in equipment will drive down operating expenses and improve product quality, and after the new investment is recovered, a new level of profit is achieved.

- Sometimes an entity has a good product line but lacks marketing expertise or merely needs to open up new markets and move into new geographic areas in order to be successful.

- Sometimes the existing employees are not competent and bringing in new managers, plus evaluating and re-training existing operations personnel will turn things around.

- Sometimes relatively small product changes and re-design, re-branding, and re-packaging of products will greatly increase the marketability of the company's product line.

You should look for a situation in which a very successful business is up for sale simply because the owner-operator-founder has reached an age at which they want to phase out and retire, but do not have any children or relatives who want to run the business. In such a case, it is sometimes possible to negotiate very favorable terms and conditions to acquire and take over the business. But the expertise and secrets of operations can remain in the head of the founder if a proper transition is not negotiated.

Financing a business acquisition can take many forms. You could of course use your own money. Sometimes people have left an existing company and taken out a sizeable 401K or a lump-sum pension buyout and used this money to buy into a business situation that opens up a new and very successful career path for them. But often it is wise to think in terms of OPM ("other people's money") in addition to your own investment. If you borrow directly from a financial institution, or solicit investment from a venture capital group, be prepared to develop a complete business plan and present it very effectively, enthusiastically selling your expertise and perspectives and the unique business opportunity. But OPM will bring controls and monitoring and reporting and sometimes an unreasonable impatience on the part of the investors.

Lastly, there is what is called the "cold start" -- namely a new business started from nothing, which often has the lowest probability of success, but also might have the highest return on investment and effort because a well-protected original idea can not only differentiate you from others, but also can start off without any direct competitors. Of course, an unconventional idea and business concept must always meet a real need in the marketplace or else it will soon fail. And a cold start requires a high degree of persistence and also deep pockets since banks are conservative and will be reluctant to underwrite a new and unproven idea, even if the principal has a lot of relevant industry experience.

Here are some examples for starting your own business.

•   If you work at a company and a new opportunity arises, but the company decides not to pursue this opportunity, then with a little negotiation and a well-prepared proposal, you might be able to obtain perpetual exclusive rights to pursue this opportunity yourself. Make sure that any legal agreement totally indemnifies you from prior company actions, and gives you perpetual exclusive rights to the concept and opportunity. Otherwise, someone in the future might come back to the idea and then compete with whatever actions and investment that you might undertake, and undermine your business.

The advantage of doing something like this is that you might have put a lot of effort into an internal business plan, market research, and analysis for a particular opportunity, and know more about the opportunity than anyone else. If this is true, and your company decides not to follow-up on the business plan, you need to obtain exclusive rights (at little or no cost) to take the idea and start your own business. If you need startup capital, think OPM (other-people's-money) and not your own, but rather emphasize that the investment that you are putting in is your own knowledge and time, and that you alone in this world have the expertise on the opportunity.

- Suppose you work for a company and they decide to outsource your work (maybe a whole department) to an outside contractor, perhaps located overseas with cheap labor. You could consider offering your company another outsourcing deal for yourself and some of your displaced co-workers, and underbid the offshore group. Your pitch would be that you know the work better than any outsource group and don't need training and can start immediately. They won't have a language problem as in many offshore outsourcing contracts. They won't have the turnover of personnel that is typical in an outsource firm. And end-users (participants) will be much more satisfied with the service. You could also offer a number of value-added services to increase your margins, especially things that an outsource-offshore group could never do, but which would be very valuable for the company. You could have a cloud-computing service provide the support platforms, so that you wouldn't have to make a big investment in infrastructure.

- If you have been involved with any "moonlight" activities outside of your primary employment, then sometimes it is an option to expand on one or more of such activities and become involved full-time. Some persons have been involved in real estate investments, either alone or with several friends and partners, and let such activities accumulate in asset value and in revenue (rental or private mortgages), and at the appropriate time become involved in such investments full-time.

- Sometimes people have been involved in hobbies for a number of years, and then convert such hobbies to full-time revenue-producing activities. Examples are travel and becoming a full-time tour director; music and becoming a full-time musician or music teacher; sports and becoming a full-time trainer or sports tutor; automobiles and opening a full-time service operation; and many other such business ventures related to former hobbies.

121

- Sometimes staff professionals, namely lawyers, accountants, engineers, and medical personnel who are currently working for a company, decide to leave and set up their own professional practice. Depending on their background, expertise, and specialties it is sometimes better to first join an existing professional practice first, and then decide to set up their own practice at a later date.

- There are endless resources to help in the decision to start your own business, or to partner with others in a business venture, and the *Appendix* includes just a few of these. Don't let the preponderance of information distract or overwhelm you. Go back to your *CareerRoadmap* and review what you want and how you plan to get there. For those with the proper disposition, self-employment is considered the ultimate career choice. Being your own boss can have great appeal -- there is nobody to fire you and you are in control of your destiny, at least to a point. Remember that you still have to positively interact with many other groups and persons to have a successful business.

****

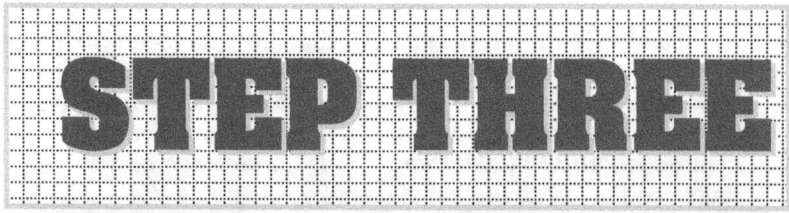

3.1 ORGANIZE TO CONTROL YOUR CAREER AND YOUR LIFE

Now is the time to not just let things happen in your life and career. Don't delay for one more day in seizing control, and stop letting yourself be bounced back-and-forth by others and false opportunities. You must be **constantly proactive** regarding your career development. You must judicially form your evolving plans, and execute actions for achievements. Remaining passive and not proactive will lead to disappointment and frustration.

To control your career, you must become **highly organized**. Namely, more organized than anyone around you or anyone you have ever met. The core of your organization will be *systems, process, preparation, practice, actions,* and *personal management*. Without this structure, attempts at organization will fail.

This section will get you started, and to do so, you need **tools and support**. The previous sections of this book have advocated the following things to structure your career control:

123

- Your *CareerRoadmap* will pull it all together and establish a path to the future. The *Core* is your *Skills, Education, and Experience*. And your first level of attention to leveraging this *Core* is *Position Management* and career *Opportunities Awareness and Development*. Your *CareerRoadmap* is maintained by orchestration of eight key elements: *(1) Information Development, (2) Contact Development, (3) Public Relations, (4) Publishing, (5) Presentations, (6) Education, (7) Certification and Licensing,* and *(8) Memberships.* You will want to automate the maintenance of the *Roadmap* and its key elements to the maximum extent possible.

- Your *Career Information System* *(Section 2.3)* consists of all information elements that can help your career. This is fed by information from online, print, email, disks, meetings, lunches and other meals, conferences, seminars, etc. and should be automated as much as possible through RSS, links, opt-ins, and subscriptions. Email feeds are also useful, such as Google Alerts. This raw information should be filtered at several levels, to weed out things that might be "nice to know" but are not relevant to your career. And this filtering should identify things that deserve immediate action, action within a week or two, or should be archived in your career information database for future reference. If something has immediate value, it then must be reviewed thoroughly, and appropriate information should be fed into the *Career Contacts* and/or the *Career Opportunities* system. And if an item is very hot, you will want to follow-up in a timely manner with letters, emails, phone calls/voicemails, as appropriate.

- Your *Career Contacts and Connections System* *(Section 2.4)* will keep track of everyone who can help your career. A prime source of these contacts is the *Career Information System*, but you also will generate useful contacts from many other sources like professional contacts at conferences, meetings, seminars, online, emails, informal discussions, social networking and even hearsay. But just like raw information, contacts must be filtered and sorted to determine the highest priority contacts and then developing and maintaining plans to nurture and "qualify" these contacts through letters, emails, voicemails, and face-to-face approaches. Some contacts will prove to be not useful or totally unresponsive after several attempts to generate some sort of interaction. And then, after evaluating and interacting with a career contact, eventually you will want to very judicially explore

124

career opportunities, using skills appropriate to the position, and the level of influence of the particular contact. Generally, you never want to ask a contact if they themselves or anybody they know have any "current job openings." Instead, you would indirectly inquire "who is building an organization" to address a particular industry opportunity, or that you yourself have been exploring "new career opportunities" in the industry, and would appreciate their perspectives.

- Your **Career Opportunity System** *(Section 2.5)* will keep track of opportunities for your career development. You will feed this *Opportunities System* from many sources, including the *Career Information System* and your *Career Contacts System.* The idea is to "keep your ear to the ground" -- both internally and externally to your current career situation. Secondly, you need to carefully and thoroughly review any potential career opportunities, and then follow up through existing or new career contacts, as appropriate. You also should be looking at career opportunities information as a source for your own potential business ventures, as well as a guide to any educational and certification activities. This *Career Opportunities System* should be keeping track of industry changes, important events, growth areas, new innovations, product and service announcements, mergers and acquisitions, key personnel changes, changes in government regulation, and/or new legislation, etc. -- which you determine will lead to career opportunities for yourself, and which deserve monitoring and follow-up.

- Your **Career Public Relations Program** *(Section 2.5)* will control what the world should know about you to further your career. The idea is to direct and control and target information about your background and accomplishments. Your don't want to be a person who unwisely "has no unspoken or unwritten thoughts." Rather, think everything through. If there is a key conference coming up in the future (a year ahead or so), you want to consider if you yourself should be a speaker, on a subject that will advance your career. And if such a situation should arise, you want to toot your horn about your involvement, and to control tightly any bio or PR releases. Similarly, if the timing is appropriate, you want to consider publishing as a PR opportunity. And internal to a current career situation, you want to make sure that the appropriate persons are aware of your accomplishments and capabilities, and consider internal publication opportunities and events and meetings as possible career PR channels. You

125

will want to make sure that your online presence is carefully thought-out and controlled and up-to-date.

- Your *"Plan-B"* and *Exit Plan* to manage career changes and emergencies *(Section 2.6)* will help you from being caught off-guard when things that you cannot control begin to shake your life. Your should be loyal and dedicated to your current career situation, but never naïve. In some companies, even the highest level executives are kept in the dark regarding organizational changes, merger-acquisitions, and traumatic financial disruptions. By developing the above *Career Systems*, you will be well-prepared to deal with the unknown. But if you know little about what is happening in the industry, and have few if any contacts outside your company, then you will be starting-from-zero if you are dislocated. Don't let yourself be among the many who are so unprepared for change.

- Your *Career Education (Section 2.14),* and *Certification, and Licensing Programs (Section 2.13)* will increase your knowledge base and affirm your competence, and keep you up-to-date in your field. This is a life-long process, and today there are many channels and venues for education and training. Refer back to the above *Sections* and to the appropriate links in the *Appendix* to refresh your career education knowledge. Everyone needs to have a lifelong *Career Education Program*, and anyone who is highly directed to seek the best career development opportunities will have a very complete *Education Program.*

Furthermore, you must look at *publishing (Section 2.10)*, *speaking (Section 2.12)* and *association memberships (Section 2.15)* as "tools" that you will use to publicize yourself, to identify contacts, and to further your knowledge base. Internally to an existing career situation, you must look at *internal meetings* and *professional interactions* as opportunities to advance your career.

Time management, *personal management*, and *prioritization* are paramount in executing your career management and control process. Again, at all costs, you must avoid "letting things happen." So one of the first things that you must do now when you finish this book is to establish and follow schedules of your activities, including career-related tasks. The next section will address scheduling as related to career control and development.

****

126

3.2 SCHEDULE AND MANAGE YOUR TIME

First, remember that schedules are merely meant to support your life activities, and help you achieve your goals and accomplishments. Do not let scheduling take on a life of its own and distract you from your goals. Some persons are so schedule driven that they lose sight of their objectives. Don't let this happen to you.

Budget time for your career including venture activities. No matter how busy you are, you must always make time for nurturing and furthering your career, and if you have undertaken any ventures, you know how important it is to schedule your time and be extremely organized. Maintaining your *CareerRoadmap*, keeping your *Career Information*, *Career Contacts*, and *Career Opportunities* systems up to date takes time, and you should automate the process to the highest extent possible. Devote time for career education, certification, publications, and presentation -- all focused on furthering your career.

Start with your ***Daily Schedule***. Put it on your computer, smartphone, or even just a convenient small spiral notepad. Establish this daily schedule the night before. When you begin this *Daily Schedule*, include everything – the time you get up, meals, dressing, travel time, etc. – namely, every detail that chews up time during the day. Your goal is to be more organized than anybody else. Be realistic and precise. When you schedule something that you have never done before, leave extra time. But if an activity is something that you know very well, try to speed up the time for completion. On every single day, including holidays and weekends, set your alarm clock. Get up early every day, even with little sleep -- you can always take a short nap later, and after one day you will catch up on your sleep. Many people find that the best time to do things is early in the morning, before any unforeseen demands arise. When you schedule your day, follow priorities, and think "career" and "control of your life" and don't just fit your career-related thinking in-between things that other people want you to do. If you get temporarily derailed from your planned schedule by unplanned items or distractions, try to return to the originally planned times as soon as possible. Of course, if something of absolutely higher priority arises unexpectedly, then you might have to re-orient your schedule. But beware of "false priorities" and remember it is OK to decline a meeting invitation that has been offered just because someone else finds it convenient for them. Be prepared to keep on schedule by deflecting lesser priority items and refusing to defer to the minutiae thrown in your way by others, but be friendly and supportive in these refusals. Lastly, on your *Daily Schedule*, strive for daily accomplishments, not merely start-and-stop and leaving a lot of things unfinished for the next day.

Here are some important points to keep in mind every day when setting up your *Daily Schedule*:

- Allocate definite time intervals each day for career-related activities, even if only 5-minutes at a time. This will include scanning the web, scanning publications, scanning email and voicemail, scanning paper mail, and so forth, as indicated in your *Career Information System*.

- Leave time to sum up career information and activities at the end of each day.

- Leave time at the end of each day to establish the schedule for the next day.

- Leave intervals during the day for career-related contact time. This time could be for outgoing phone calls, outgoing voicemails and emails, or drafting contact letters. But don't be rushed into anything that is not well prepared and thought-out. Prepare thoroughly any communication, but especially any real-time phone calls.

- Prioritize every daily activity - ask yourself what is the most important thing for your career, both short-term and long-term. Don't let busy-work and curiosity get in the way of more important things. Above all, don't aimlessly scan web job sites to "see what is out there."

- Keep everything absolutely organized. Don't gather information and contacts only to lose track of "when, what, where" so that your valuable career research time is wasted.

Some pointers:

- Get things into an electronic form. Incorporate automation and aids and tools like RSS, email filters, bots, and so forth. If you are not familiar with these automated online information management aids, research the Web through a search engine.

- Don't ever pile papers on a desk or table, or cabinet. If they are important enough to save, they are important enough to file in organized hanging folders. Printed publications should be saved on shelves in your personal library.

- No matter how small your house or apartment, your career is important enough to devote space to a desk area, a file cabinet, and a bookcase, if not a separate private personal office.

- As an exercise in time management, try doing things in half the time, but maintain quality. At first it might seem impossible. You can start with simple things like brushing your teeth, taking a shower, getting dressed.

- When you think of something of higher priority than what you are currently doing, interrupt what you are doing and go right to what you thought of.

- If you multitask, don't let a lesser priority interrupt a higher priority item.

- Go to sleep earlier, even 5 minutes, and set your alarm 5 minutes earlier.

- When you sit down at your desk, review your daily schedule before starting the first thing that comes to mind.

There are many, many "time management" references, publications, and courses, and most of these focus around keeping a schedule. Many readers will be highly aware of such sources and might already be keeping a schedule. But for those who would like to refresh themselves on the subject of time management, you should research the Web in a controlled and directed manner. Now beyond your *Daily Schedule*, here are some additional scheduling guidelines.

1.   Keep a **_Weekly Schedule_**, day-by-day including weekends and holidays. Look ahead for the week and carefully schedule meetings as needed, tasks that must be completed, people to contact, family time and obligations, recreational activities, etc. Include details and schedule hour-by-hour as much as possible to insure that your time is managed carefully. But be realistic. Try to strive for completing all tasks in priority order. Do not over-schedule yourself but make sure that the most important things are accomplished on time. Get out of the habit of making endless

lists of tasks but then accomplishing little on the list and then re-working and adding to the list. This is useless and chews up valuable time. Instead, plan each week carefully and work the plan very closely. Aim for a number of weekly accomplishments. And at the end of the week, schedule time for debriefing yourself so that you can understand why any goals for the week were not met, and also to add up and admire what you have accomplished in the week.

2.   You will also need a ***Monthly Schedule***, but this does not need to be as detailed as a weekly hour-by-hour schedule. Look ahead and don't miss anything important, like a conference, event, meeting, or opportunities that could affect your career. Remember the rule that you must be proactive to control your life and career, and not just let things happen or be constantly chasing things determined by others. Put things that you yourself initiate at the highest priority.

3.   Next, keep a ***Yearly Schedule***. On this, you also must keep track of upcoming conferences, events, meetings, or opportunities that could affect your career, both positively and negatively. Your will be linking this *Yearly Schedule* with your *Career Information*, *Career Contacts*, and *Career Opportunities* databases. Again, be proactive, and emphasize what you initiate and control in your life and career. The further you go out in time, the more your schedules should reflect what you yourself control, what you initiate, and with your own priorities at the top.

4.   Your ***CareerRoadmap*** is basically your total-life plan beyond the current year. But it is useful to establish a ***Multiple Year Schedule***, encompassing the next 5-10 years. For example, list things like planned vacation trips, planned career changes, planned multiple-year educational activities, educational benchmarks for children, and so forth.

Some people incorrectly think that the way to advance their career is to be a workaholic, devoting as much time as possible to their job, to the exclusion of family, friends, or other activities. This is usually the opposite of the reality. Who would you yourself hire to work for you, a person who works long hours or a person who is very organized and knowledgeable, keeps a strict schedule, and always gets things done on time?

130

The time you invest in your family and friends will pay you back if you nurture a two-way relationship. Namely, "I support you 100% but expect you to also support me 100%." It is well from time to time to have a family meeting to hear their issues and to express your support and to clarify your schedule. Career development takes time, but you must arrange your schedule to assure adequate time for your spouse, family and friends, and professional associates and your key contacts.

****

3.3 *WORKING YOUR CONTACTS AND CONNECTIONS*

In *Section 2.4*, the need for your *Career Contacts and Connections System* was introduced, with a number of details and a suggested electronic structure in spreadsheet form. In this section, we will expand on this, with information on how you should follow up and manage contacts.

Contacts are a primary source for you to expand your career. If handled properly, contacts can lead to job opportunities without any competition from other candidates, and permit you to totally bypass the mostly miserable and misleading online job listings and even most of the human resources process. But of course you must have developed yourself as a unique and very hot property in the industry, through the self-development processes described in this *Guide*, including your career marketing and public relation process.

Any career contact or connection must be treated as a very valuable item for your career and your life. Therefore, how you follow-up and nurture any contact is of high importance. You do not want to overlook a connection or contact or discard either because you are "too busy" or make a purely arbitrary judgment about the importance of the contact without any substantive information. For example, you might be introduced to a person who initially comes across as not well-dressed, not articulate and you don't know their title or position, so you don't strike up a conversation or get any information. Only later, you could find out that they were a key individual in the industry, and you missed a chance to establish a relationship.

As mentioned back in *Section 2.4*, contacts and connections arise from many sources and circumstances. Some will be face-to-face, others out of publications and online sources, and many will arise out of proactive actions that you initiate. Many contacts will flow from sources in your *Career Information System*. And others will arise from connections you already have through family, friends, alumni associations, fellow students, professional societies, trade groups, and prior career situations. But wherever a contact may arise, your steps in qualifying and for following up and nurturing a contact should follow a strict sequence. Just to review, these steps are:

1. Identification: Obtaining as much relevant information on the contact, such as name, title, organization, physical address, email, telephone, associations, etc.

2. Ranking: Assigning a priority for this contact. Key industry players will rank high, as will anyone who is currently or might be in the future creating new career positions, but even peers or subordinates who are reliable and knowledgeable could have a high ranking.

3. Qualification: This is the process of initially interacting with the contact (in writing, electronically, or face-to-face), and obtaining responses that will tell you if they are a valuable career resource, can be trusted, have unique industry knowledge and eventually place high value on your own knowledge, perspectives, and therefore would work well with you in a career position in their organization. Keep away from anything public or quasi-public (that is, not private and secure) and don't ever send career contact emails from a work location or a work-provided mobile device. Tweets, blogs, and faxes are also security problems and should never be used for any qualification or nurturing initiatives. It goes without saying that this whole qualification process must be done very diplomatically and indirectly, so that you do not spoil the contact situation but definitely determine up front if this contact is of value and reliable and trustworthy.

4. Filtering: This consists of the process of eliminating contacts who do not respond to your qualification overtures, or respond negatively to your initiatives, or prove to be unreliable sources of information, or present particular security problems. One exception is key players who are "very busy" and often will not respond to your efforts until you yourself have established a key career position and can offer them more advantages than they themselves enjoy.

5. Nurturing: This is the process of interacting with a qualified contact in order to further your career in a variety of ways. This interaction is a two-way street, so be prepared to offer knowledge, insight, and perspectives that could help the contact, and in return you will find out about what is going on in various segments of the industry. You can inquire about the contact's reaction to some new event or product or innovation, some new regulation or legislation, or their opinions about a company. And eventually you can inquire about career opportunities in their organization or a different organization. Of course, there are many cautions to guide

133

the nurturing process. The sections which follow will help you in this regard.

Contacts from Publications and Online Postings

Innate to your *Career Information System*, you will be keeping up with the industry, and will be reading both online and print publications. When you see names of persons of interest, make sure that you enter them into your *Career Contacts System* and database. If the name is the author of an article, immediately think of how you might contact them with comments on their article or book, in a manner which shows that you know what you are talking about, and have knowledge and perspectives on the industry. Prioritize this contact, with a ranking system of your choosing. Save the article electronically or file it in an organized paper file, with linking so that you can associate it with the contact name. But, do not contact them until you fit them in the priority rankings of contacts, since there might be a more important contact that deserves more immediate follow up.

If only the author's name is supplied, you must write to the editor or publisher with a short note to be passed along to the actual author. Alternatively, the editor or publisher might have been authorized to release an email address or even a physical address. In this note or email you will congratulate them on the article or book, offer a few cogent but pertinent and carefully worded comments, and pose at least one question about which you would value their thoughts, in order to get a return response and learn more about them and get further contact information about them. A few guidelines for such an initial note:

- You could compare their ideas in this article to previous articles or works of theirs, and comment on the importance of their perspectives to the industry. And you should demonstrate your knowledge and "bring value to the discussion." If you have ever written articles on the subject of their article, make reference to your own publications and don't be afraid to "toot your horn."

- You could elicit their thoughts regarding some new or proposed regulation or legislation that will impact the industry.

- You could compare their ideas to the works and proposals of others, in a favorable light.

- You could offer your support for furthering their point of view throughout the industry, and even mention some specific possible actions.

- You should always briefly identify yourself, what you do, and your perspective, and even a bit of your background and experience, but do not identify your current organization or career situation. If you send an email, it of course should be from a home computer (NEVER from a work computer) and from a secure email address that you have specifically set up for this purpose.

- You should of course include complete contact information (only home location) for yourself.

- In case the article or book identifies their current organization, and includes a biography, you should not have any trouble obtaining information to send them this note or email.

- You should completely avoid any controversial or political statements, personal philosophies, and religious or other ideologies, and be careful about throwing your opinions around when you don't really know this person. And when they might respond to your note, don't be drawn into such topics by this contact. Remember that they might even be testing you out to see your own point-of-view.

- Above all, in such an initial overture, NEVER mention anything about careers, jobs, or vacancies, and NEVER include a resume or biography, but you might include a reference to your functional capabilities and experience, such as "...having been in the industry for ___ years, I have had much experience in _____ ..."

Contacts from Face-to-Face Introductions

Everyone that you meet at a trade fair, convention, or conference, or in a course or seminar, or in a meeting (both internal and external), or on travel, or socially, or at sports events, or through clubs and associations, or through family, friends and neighbors, should be treated as a potential career contact. You should develop your ability to remember names and faces, and should diplomatically try to get as much information about those that you meet in real time.

135

Here are some pointers in leveraging and following up on face-to-face introductions:

- Always carry your own business cards (or generic cards without company affiliation, as appropriate), and offer a business card with the intention of getting a card back from the contact. If they have no card, ask them to please write their name and contact information on the back of one of your own cards.

- In real time after being introduced, become adept at making favorable comments about the person, trying to find out who they are and how they respond to personal interaction. You might even make a comment about some event or trend or happening of mutual interest.

- Shortly after meeting this contact, send off an email or a written letter. If this person appears to be a key contact, take the time to find a private location and send them an email from a smartphone, being careful about what you say, but keeping it short. Then follow up later with a longer message or letter, in order to begin the nurturing, cultivation, and filtering process.

- When introduced face-to-face don't be misled by appearances or demeanor. Some key contacts might not come across very positively initially, and some very capable people are naturally shy and lacking in social skills. Also some key people are naturally rude, but can end up being a good contact and well worth the overhead factor. So it is best to always react positively and not be drawn into any negative or inappropriate comments when introduced.

- You often need to be proactive and persistent in making face-to-face contact in a real-time situation. After a key individual has spoken at a conference, often the speakers' platform is rushed with attendees eager to make contact, introduce themselves, and obtain follow-up contact and/or address information. Sometimes it is best to follow the speaker out after the crowd has dispersed and politely introduce yourself appropriately. Also at a conference, the conference managers will often have a list of attendees available, including contact information that has been authorized and released by each person, but to obtain the list requires extra effort.

- When you go to a meeting, get there early and introduce yourself to anyone that you don't already know and obtain contact information and business cards. Make sure that whoever is running the meeting passes around a "sign-in sheet" and get a copy of this sheet. Make special note of key individuals and high level persons and officers. Follow up after the meeting with appropriate media and contact information.

Contacts and Connections from Announcements and Events

Both online and in electronic or print media, you will find a constant stream of announcements of executive changes, appointments, and promotions, as well as reporting of mergers and acquisitions, new office and facility locations, new products and services, new legislation, regulations, creation of governmental organizations, panels, and study groups. Also, don't overlook the information contained in advertisements, which often indicates the intent and strategy of an organization. You want to sharpen your awareness of career implications when you encounter such items. And you want to become very adept at creatively realizing how you can utilize such announcements and events to help your career development.

Here are a few ways that you can utilize announcements and reported events.

- When a promotion or appointment is reported in a newspaper, in a magazine, online, on TV, or otherwise, often the person will be facing new challenges and could be a contact to whom you could send a note of congratulations, generically mentioning your experience and background, and offering a few comments on your perspectives which could be utilized to help meet the new challenges.

- Similarly, when a new business venture or product or service announcement is released, companies are often hoping to expand business, and you could look up the company online, find the names of the head of sales or the marketing vp in either an online link or in their annual report (often an online PDF file), and write to them through the company's headquarters address or merely call the company's main number (found through their website or through sites like Yahoo finance), and ask the operator for their office or their location.

- If there is a merger-acquisition that has been announced, of course one of the first considerations is that jobs will be lost in at least the acquired company, and also fewer in the acquiring company. But in addition, this is an indication of a change in operations and strategies, and often the PR releases will have names and responsibilities mentioned and these people are possible contacts for you to identify yourself and state what you can do for them in this transition period and also to lead and assist as they alter their strategies and pursue new business opportunities.

- When new regulation or legislation has been proposed and/or actually passed, this signals changes in the industry, and companies often need help in adapting or taking advantage or the new environment. If you have capabilities and experience relevant to the matter, send off correspondence to the appropriate officers or departments of companies that will be affected.

- When new government procurement contracts or requests for bid proposals are announced, opportunities will arise for companies in the particular area. Those who get in early often have excellent career opportunities. The industry segments could be related to the environment, natural resources (mining, oil, gas), agriculture, education, etc. and in the initial stage or such activities, consultants, and executive leaders with the proper experience are needed to define the opportunities.

- The Internet is such a vast real-time global information network, that you need to set up alerts and filters to keep in touch with events and news that could generate career contacts and connections. You need to develop your creative capabilities for doing this.

Lunch and the Power Lunch

Lunch meetings have for a long time been a venue for cultivating contacts. This is often a good format for discussing important

138

business mixed with socializing and some relaxation. But for your career development, you always want to manage lunches carefully. It is OK to have lunch occasionally with peers, but do not let this become a socializing habit which impinges on your career development. You should schedule lunches with your boss, and even coordinate lunches with several levels above (your boss included) for a "working meeting" over lunch to address a particular matter. Treat these just as you would in setting up and coordinating any meeting on an important subject.

Remember that in cultivating contacts that you have to constantly assess the desire to "be popular" among peers, with the desire to build relationships with those that can help your career, including people both within and outside of your current organization. It is good to have a goal of lunching with several persons each month who are key in the industry outside your current organization, and have valuable perspectives and high accomplishments. (Note that if these individuals happen to be working for a competitor, you must be very, very careful of security in having lunch with them.) Another luncheon goal is to meet at least once per month with one or more new contacts, and not just the "same-old, you-again" closed circle.

Regarding the "power lunch" which is often an expensive lunch in a high-profile restaurant, trying to impress a particular contact -- this should be considered carefully. Often such locations are highly publicized and if you want to be seen with a particular person that is OK, but others will see you and react in kind, and also you might experience both interruptions from others as well as "table-jumping" on the part of others who want to disrupt your power lunch or use the opportunity to meet your key contact without having to pick up the tab. So be careful and often you will want to choose a lunch location that does not present such problems, but will impress the contact. For key consultants or executives, try to find out their favorite lunch locations or their particular culinary desires -- don't make the mistake of choosing a location for which they have a dislike or a cuisine which they will not eat. Of course, don't try to have a power lunch at a noisy location that will be disruptive and annoying. And don't overlook having lunch brought in to a particular executive office or in-house location for a time-efficient lunch but tastefully done and not just an "eat-and-run" situation. Lastly, in some industries, a "fun lunch" in the park served from one of the many sometimes exotic lunch trucks is just what is needed to make the right impression, and being creative about a power lunch could add to establishing yourself as an innovator. And sometimes a "nutrition lunch" and a health walk will be appropriate.

You need to develop a circle of supporters and key contacts who join you either alone or with a few others for lunch on a regular basis. For this purpose, you need to keep a calendar and work the overhead factor in proportion to the career value. You will support each other, but you will be careful about giving away key contacts of your own, many of whom you should protect carefully.

Lastly, remember your goals in cultivating and nurturing contacts. Be careful of naïve trust in individuals who might be key in the industry but will play one person against another, or are just looking for "inside information" to put in some column or leverage to their own narrow advantage. Beware or charlatans who know little but have become expert at pretending and picking the brains of others, and who will plagiarize and misrepresent, and could quote anything you say or write, often out of context and distorted.

Don't ever pester or harass or overwork a contact -- your goal is to nurture and cultivate and make a positive impression. But remember that some key individuals are very busy and might never respond to your overtures, but should be kept on your list of contacts, and that at least you might be putting your name and information before their eyes, and perhaps they will pass something off to another person, so don't give up on them. And sometimes it is wise to hold back on reaching out to a potential contact until you can bring definite value to the table and have more to offer in a discussion.

The Contact Bottom Line: Is There A Career Position?

Eventually you will get to the point where you will want to explore if any of your career contacts that you have identified, developed, and nurtured can be a direct link to a career position. This is one major element of the bottom line in utilizing your contacts, but it is not the only element. Some of your contacts can help your career in many ways but do not have any direct link to job opportunities, and should be kept active but never tapped for information on career positions.

Remember the guidance given in *Section 2.7* on always having a "Plan-B" and an Exit Strategy. One of the reasons for cultivating your career contacts on an ongoing basis is to have people and situations that you can always refer to immediately in unforeseen situations, so that you never have to "start from zero" when considering

140

employment moves. But most of the time, you will want to control your career and your life so that you are entirely in control of the timing and planning of career development actions.

Here are some of the ways of broaching the subject of career positions in a carefully managed manner.

- You can send off letters to some of your contacts who have been certified and nurtured and are trusted, stating that you are now exploring career position changes, and are interested if they are aware of openings in their organization or other organizations. But be very careful of the wording. Do not attach a resume at this point, and do not refer to any online job listings that you might have seen. Be sure to review your background and capabilities, even if previously this contact has been made highly aware of your background and experience. No matter how eager you are to look for an opening, never sound desperate or demanding. You might want to do this one-contact-at-a-time, because if you are given some direct leads for hiring managers and you never respond, this particular contact might be "spoiled" for any future use.

- You can send out generic "PR releases" on your capabilities to a wider list, and/or change your Facebook, Linkedin, and other online social network postings. But be careful. You do not want to state that "you are now available for new career opportunities" unless you are between jobs or that your current position is being eliminated. Again, never include a resume at this point, and be careful of any wider "broadcast" like this, and be highly aware of security and privacy concerns.

- You can more humbly choose one of your most closely trusted contacts to act as your "advisor" regarding a career position change, and mention that you value their great experience and their special perspectives, and would appreciate their advise and guidance as you move to a new career position. Summarize your background and experience, and do everything to help them help you, but do not send a resume, because even this person might decide to merely forward your resume to some manager or an HR type without all of the needed background and guidance.

141

- If one of your contacts gives you the names of hiring managers to call, who might or might not have current defined and approved vacancies, you need to proceed very carefully. Don't get so excited that you pick up the phone immediately and end up in a brief conversation that deteriorates into the "supposed hiring manager" requesting a resume and then ending the call without you being able to "tell your story." In such a case you will often end up in a pile of resumes, competing with other candidates in a long and often senseless lottery-type process.

- Sometimes the best situation is when there is no currently defined open position at all, but when an officer or authorized executive understands your capabilities, your demonstrated accomplishments, and your experience, plus a clear statement of what new opportunities you can develop for the organization – then you have a great deal possible. Such an authorized person can immediately bring you in on a contract, with a good chance of joining the staff permanently if their judgment pans out. Of course, if this is what happens, you must perform superbly while you are "on trial," even exceeding their expectations. If you have the self-confidence to proceed in a situation like this, then you can diplomatically suggest to the proper contact person that such an arrangement be set up.

****

3.4 *LEVERAGING YOUR CAREER OPPORTUNITIES*

As described in *Section 2.5*, career opportunities could arise and be identified via a variety of sources. When you identify something new as a career opportunity possibility, you need to follow the steps described in *Section 2.5* to get the information into an organized and accessible form. There are three ways to think of and to categorize career opportunities:

1. *Internal Career Opportunities*: Situations that arise or are proactively prompted by yourself within your current organization.

2. *External Career Opportunities*: Situations that arise outside of your current organization, for example things originating with competitors, or because of governmental, regulatory, legislative or environmental changes, or because of innovations and changes in technology.

3. *Venture Opportunities*: Situations that arise because of innovations, actions of others, or even ideas which you have originated.

This *Section 3.4* is included to provide guidance on leveraging career opportunities which you might identify. After you have evaluated and filtered a career opportunity, if it passes your established criteria, you need to generate at least a "mini" career opportunity business plan, following the guidance given in *Section 2.2*.

Whether the career opportunity is either internal or external to your current organization, doing at least a mini business case will help you assess the elements of your decision process, including estimating the financial impact and career path implications. Some of the things that you will be asking yourself about a potential career opportunity are:

- Does the career opportunity open new doors for yourself, or, despite being lucrative and a seemingly attractive situation, does this opportunity narrow your future options, and eventually make you less viable in the career marketplace?

- Will the career opportunity place you in an organization that is now "legacy" or on the road to being legacy, namely might seem "safe" at this time, and even deemed a "core competency" at this time, but is not linked to the future of the organization or the industry.

- If either an internal or external opportunity will require new training on your part, how extensive will this training be, and will this particular training add to your general capabilities or is it rather narrow training that will push you into a career specialty that you never intended to pursue.

- Can a seeming career opportunity be vulnerable to outsourcing, namely is there a rather routine aspect to the opportunity?

- Are there any key industry players involved with this career opportunity? If it is a new venture, are there any important and trusted investors, who themselves would have done a thorough business case?

The above are mostly cautions for you to keep in mind when embarking on a mini business plan for a career opportunity. Now let us look at the positive aspects and actions that you can take to leverage an identified and screened career opportunity.

Career Opportunity Leveraging Preparation

When you have identified a possible career opportunity and collected associated information and filtered and evaluated the opportunity, and at least drafted a mini business case for it, you are then in a position to consider how the opportunity can be properly leveraged into your *Career Business Plan* and your *CareerRoadmap*. Go back to these career systems and review your education, experience, skills, and accomplishments, and also review your persona and perspectives, and see how the opportunity under consideration aligns with all of these elements.

When you have done the above, you are ready to now consider how to leverage a possible opportunity.

Leveraging Internal Career Opportunities

If there is an internal job announcement for a particular career opportunity, you can expect competition from both internal and external candidates, and in fact it might be too late once the vacancy announcement is out, since the job might already be "hard-wired" for a favored candidate or someone that an officer level has selected. If the hard-wired candidate is yourself, then congratulations -- you have been working your internal contacts and internal career marketing and career PR properly.

But if there has simply been an internal announcement of a new area of business, or a new officer level, or a new person brought in to head an existing or new operation, then you need to evaluate the situation as indicated per the previous guidelines in this *Section 3.4*, and then proceed as follows.

- Inquire through your internal trusted contacts regarding any news or hearsay that is related to this internal change, but always place a reliability factor on the information.

- Schedule lunch with several of your internal contacts, and elicit their reaction to the internal change or event which has precipitated this possible career opportunity.

- Intensify your career marketing and PR program elements. This is a good time to get an article in an internal company publication.

- Send emails, carefully worded, to trusted internal contacts, with your thoughts about the new business opportunities for the company, associated with the event or change that has occurred. Be aware that anything you send is subject to viewing by others, so never make any disparaging comments, only a positive perspective that will demonstrate your realization of new business, new revenues, and new profits for the company.

- Only when you have learned more and crafted a plan and strategy should you then consider asking your direct management about any new career opportunities that might be associated with the internal event or change. You can ask your management if they wouldn't mind if you inquired further internally about this change. This way, you put them on notice that you intend to be proactive in exploring opportunities. But be careful. Some managers are very defensive and if they are "control freaks" their reaction to such an inquiry could be negative or damaging. But if they are a supporting type of manager, they might even offer suggestions or offer to inquire up the line themselves on your behalf. Remember that by taking this action you have tipped your hand and must be prepared to play out the result.

Leveraging External Career Opportunities

When you hear about industry situations that could open up career opportunities, there are many ways that you can react. Of course, you need to proceed with high security and careful confidentiality, sometimes using a pseudonym or a proxy or a management consultant (headhunter) as a go-between initially. Even being seen with someone from a competitive organization, at a conference or at a restaurant or otherwise, could prejudice your current career position. If anything should bounce-back to your current management, this could derail your career position. But when you have established yourself as a very valuable person in the industry, and regularly speak at conferences and are yourself regarded as a key player in the industry, then you will have the self-esteem and self-confidence to be able to handle any negative reactions in your current position. In fact, in some organizations, if they know that you are "looking around," then you could be offered some enhancement to stay in your current organization, like a promotion or a compensation increase, provided that you are a highly valued key player in the organization.

The first thing that you need to do about an industry event that might open up external career opportunities is to fully research the opportunity, and gather and filter all relevant information, per the guidelines discussed in *Sections 2.3, 2.4* and *2.5*, including tapping one or more of your career contacts to get their reactions. External career opportunities can be triggered by actions of competitors, or because of governmental, regulatory, legislative or environmental changes, or because of innovations and changes in technology, so you need to be very flexible and open in researching an external opportunity. If the possible opportunity continues to be of interest after this initial research, then you will want to craft a mini business case on the opportunity.

Sometimes you will want to move very fast when an external event triggers a possible opportunity. But you can only move fast if you

146

already have the educational background, the skills, experience, and accomplishments to fit with this external opportunity. It also helps to have some contacts who are related in some way to this particular opportunity. But moving fast can have advantages and get you out in front of the crowd and get you a meeting with those associated with the possible external opportunity. Obviously you must be in a position to help in developing and assuring the success of an external activity – namely "bring something to the table" and make them feel they need to have someone of your capabilities on board for the new situation.

The focus of this entire *Guide* regarding external career opportunities is that unsolicited proposals are much more likely to land you an attractive career position than merely "applying for a job" either online or through ads or contacts. An unsolicited proposal can put you in the drivers seat and if handled right, will exclude other candidates, and keep you out of the lottery-like disarray and delays associated with the typical hiring process. You of course will need to show that you are the best and only person who can make things happen successfully for this opportunity.

In fact, some external opportunities can be generated by your own actions rather than any specific event. But such actions need to be carefully planned and executed. You do not want to send an unsolicited proposal to more than one entity or contact at a time, and you often will have to proceed through a pseudonym, or anonymously, or through a trusted "broker" or representative, in order to protect yourself. Management consultants (headhunters) can sometimes play this role. If you are clumsy at making an unsolicited proposal, the wrong person could somehow find out where you are currently working and either deliberately derail you or stupidly contact your current organization, so proceed accordingly.

Just a few points to get you going on researching and pursuing external career opportunities:

- Don't "chase" everything you see. Remain disciplined and directed, and concentrate on developing your own talents and desires, as they match your own defined persona and goals. Research and pursue external career opportunities only as they fit your established criteria.

- When you see news of some company-specific event, innovation, or announcement which you believe could open up career opportunities, you first need to find more about the company. Sometimes, they will offer "press-kit" materials as part of their company communications, and you should obtain any such materials. Also, consult their annual report(s) and any related financial documents. Also, sometimes financial analysts have reviewed their prospects related to a particular event, but some analyst reports have a high price tag. You should also of course research them through one or more online search engines, and visit their website, and contact their public relations departments for anything available. And you may find through searching that some online blogs contain opinions and hearsay. If the source is a governmental entity, follow a similar type of initial research.

- Venture capital firms often will release announcements of innovations and startups that they are backing and for which they have provided seed money. This will give you leads on possible career opportunities.

- A final caution: Although you need to be aware of changes in your industry and any other industry that you choose to monitor, make sure that you do not let this activity distract you from immediate attention to maintaining your current career position, as was discussed in *Section 2.1*.

Leveraging New Business and Venture Opportunities

Section 2.18 discussed many aspects of new business and venture opportunities, as related to your career planning. This section will expand on some actions and strategies for pursuing such career opportunities.

One strategy many would-be entrepreneurs have is to "keep their day job" and start a venture or another business on the side, and then when the venture grows up, they can quit their day job and take over the venture full-time. But this is not easy to do. It requires a great deal of organization, discipline, and time management. However, this is often a valid scenario to build into your *CareerRoadmap* and *Career Business Plan*. Before going further on this subject, it is a good idea to go back to *Section 2.18* and review the material on ventures and running your own business, including consulting applicable references in the *Appendix*.

Now, here are some suggestions for leveraging venture and business opportunities.

- A venture or self-controlled business need not be a direct follow-on to your current career position, although this might help. But of course, such a venture should not be in conflict with your current position, and of course should not violate any non-compete agreements you might have signed in the past. But remember that non-compete agreements almost always have an expiration time limit, after which you are free to operate a competing business on your own. But you almost never will be able to use any patent or trademark or proprietary information or assets from a previous position. Undertaking a legal challenge to any patent agreement or non-compete agreement is not recommended, but sometimes has been won by individuals and has been the basis for them getting control of some intellectual property, which then wins them venture capital funding.

- A venture or self-controlled business should be related at least to some avocation or hobby or skill or talent that you possess and have been involved with for a number of years. That is, never think that you can jump into an entirely new area of business just because you have a high level of motivation and enthusiasm about some idea that you have heard about. The risk of failure will be very high in such a case. You cannot "learn by doing" in any competitive environment and expect to succeed, given all of the other factors which you will have to manage. You also cannot "buy your way in" to an entirely unknown area with some money that you have saved up or have obtained from another source. Franchise training helps, but might not be very comprehensive for the real world.

- If there is a family business that you have an opportunity to take over and leave your corporate position, this might be a great opportunity, but you must remember that you have many options in addition to your running of the business yourself. For example, you could: (1) Sell the business to someone else, or (2) Hire someone to manage the business, but remain the owner and keep the profits, or (3) Expand and greatly improve the business by obtaining new investors after a complete business plan is prepared, or (4) If there is anything proprietary and which is of high value, you could license this off to someone else, or (5) You could outsource some or most of the operations, but retain a holding company which securely controls the heart of the business and prevents anyone else from copying the products and services.

These are merely three leveraging examples to get you thinking about an action plan for ventures and your own business. As an exercise, you should make a list of other leveraging ideas that come to mind, and how these ideas should be analyzed and migrated into decision points and action plans.

****

3.5 GET GOING NOW: FOCUS ON FOUR STARTING STEPS

You have worked your way through this *Guide* and have been stimulated to think about many aspects of your life and career. You have gone through many online and paper resources to build your career information base. Now you must STOP the researching and analysis, pull it all together, and put it to work.

Focus on *four fundamental elements*. Call this your PKPA Program:

⇒**PUBLICITY** – Telling the world who you are and what you have done and can do. You will maintain the utmost security and protection in control of your message. You will do this via a well-balanced and coordinated communications process as follows.

- You will publish articles in relevant magazines, journals, internal publications, making sure that your bio and picture are included, but will manage personal information as appropriate to the publication.

- You will write and circulate white papers to a select group of professional comrades and industry associates, but again manage personal information appropriately.

- You will offer comments in online blogs and reviews of online articles.

- You will give talks at conferences of major industry trade groups and at selected specialized conferences and trade shows.

- You will offer self-initiated internal talks – such as "lunchtime" sessions on key topics or on an article that you have recently published.

- You will present at alumni association meetings and at meetings of professional societies to which you belong.

- At trade shows and industry events, you will take a proactive role and consider presentation opportunities, and you will circulate among, and socialize with, attendees.

151

⇒**KNOWLEDGE** – Assessing and constantly building and improving what you know; innovating and establishing your own ideas and approaches; and protecting all that you know and develop.

- You will develop and maintain a reading program covering the important publications and journals in your field -- especially covering the important historical works that you should be familiar with and be able to quote from (and might have previously overlooked) and also the most recent ground-breaking and influential articles and books.

- Your will constantly update your *Career Information System*, your *Career Contacts System*, and your *Career Opportunities System*.

- You will take advantage of the efficiency of online learning resources, including the many online webinars that are available, and even initiate a webinar yourself. You will enroll in courses and seminars on a selective basis, keeping in mind your time-management program.

- You will meet face-to-face with both internal and external associates and influential persons, by inviting them to lunch or dinner or for a cup of coffee, and listen to what they have to say about some recent development in the field or one of their recent accomplishments which you admire.

- You will maintain a daily routine to check a carefully selected series of websites and news sources for items of relevance, automating this with RSS links, alerts, prompts, and information filters as much as possible.

⇒**PLANNING** – Being extremely organized and persistent, managing your time, keeping records, developing a living *CareerRoadmap* and highly organized *Career Systems*.

- You will set up a highly organized *Career Information System*, a highly organized *Career Contact System*, and a highly organized *Career Opportunities System*. You will break any old habits of keeping random and disorganized records which are impossible to review and update quickly. You will mechanize and make electronic these *Career Systems*, and incorporate in your time-management process tasks and events for updating these *Systems*.

- You will check monthly with your *Roadmap* to see if updates are required, to assure that your goals are in accord with your master plan, and to measure your progress

- You will keep your *Roadmap* locked up in a safe place, with other important records

- You will keep daily, monthly, and annual schedules, and check off and update your list of accomplishments. You will make time management paramount in order to adhere to these schedules, but you will revise schedules in a realistic manner, to maintain priorities.

⇒**ACTION** – Converting the above three items, in a timely manner, in priority order, to final accomplishments. To assure positive and proactive actions, you will proceed as follows.

- You will stop immediately the habit of sending out resumes at random to supposed "jobs" that are posted on the Internet or advertised in print. You will never send a resume or a job inquiry to a career contact, but rather will aim at impressing career contacts with your knowledge, accomplishments, motivation, and persistence, and professional persona, such that they will keep you in mind for career positions that are created, and they will take actions that you have stimulated through your nurturing and persistence.

- You will develop an ability to decisively reach conclusions, avoiding equivocation and aware of the dangers of "analysis paralysis". You will therefore constantly work at improving your decision-making processes.

- You will take proactive responsibility for your career, and never just "let things happen" in the job market or in a current career position. You will develop contingency plans, including a "Plan-B" to handle unforeseen career environment changes.

- You will grow eager to add to your list of life accomplishments by converting plans to completion.

- You will remain constantly aware of the need for you to convert anger and frustration to a motivating force that drives actions.

- You will learn to take little steps at a time which will build momentum

You might have been taking notes as you went through this *Prevail, Excel: Career Control Guide*. If so, go back and review those notes. If not, go back and do a quick re-read and take notes of any kind that suits you. Then answer any questions that you may have jotted down.

You might have listed a number of things that you always wanted to do in your life. But you must decide what kind of person you want to be, and what you want to do in your life, and then develop a plan to accomplish what you want. This is not just something to do when you finish chores around the house, or fit in between TV programs or golf or jogging.

****

3.6 BECOMING VERY MOTIVATED AND VERY PERSISTENT

Beware of falling into the trap of letting events and the actions of others determine what you do in life. Set your own priorities and goals and adhere to these with persistence. Make time-management a permanent habit as natural as eating and sleeping.

You should constantly reaffirm, support, and strengthen your own self-esteem and motivation. But do not become narcissistic and oblivious to the needs and desires of others around you. The *Appendix* includes a number of references that will help and inspire you in this regard.

Here are some particular things to keep in mind regarding affirming and maintaining a *high level of motivation*:

- Start every task or brainstorming exercise in a positive manner. Do not ever start off by saying *"What can go wrong"* but rather *"What can I do that is unique and will be successful because I have had many successes before"* and *"I am a winner and will win at this task"* and *"Because of my perspective and persistence, I always find a solution."* Even privately compose and write out or memorize personal "affirmations" to remind yourself of your capabilities and knowledge and accomplishments.

- Maintain your knowledge base for everything you do. Knowing what is going on and knowing how to quickly locate relevant information will make you confident that you can take on even the most difficult tasks. This confidence will support your motivation.

- Keep impeccable files and databases. If you cannot find information readily you could lose confidence and be de-motivated.

- Never start a task without having an end in mind, including a schedule to reach this end. Having a direction for every task

155

will increase your motivation. Remember that lack of clarity because of the lack of knowledge and direction is always a de-motivator.

- Always work tasks to completion, avoiding unnecessary perfectionism, but insisting on the highest standards of quality appropriate to the task. Leaving things unfinished will cause you a sense of being overloaded and this will drag down your motivation.

- Do not make long "to-do" lists and then achieve only a few things on the list. Rather, make short lists, with things in strict priority order, and then accomplish everything on the list in a timely manner.

- Place emphasis and priority on your own ideas and perspectives. Work from the "50-50" rule that at least 50% of what you do in life follows from your own initiative, leaving 50% or less to be the desires and orders of bosses, family, and friends.

- As you become more and more organized, you will gradually develop the ability to do multitasking, but without sacrificing quality, and always adhering to priorities and maintaining schedules. This high degree of organization goes hand-in-hand with high motivation.

- Motivate yourself in a stress-free manner. Stress shuts down creativity and causes mental blocks and limits your problem-solving capability. Deal with others without discord and contention. There is a time for confrontation, but use it sparingly and carefully.

- You should also review your personal appearance, dress, and persona as it affects your motivation and self-esteem. You must be genuine and honest but do not discount the relationship between how you look, how you feel, and how you act.

There is a saying *"a place for everything and everything in its place"* and this is applicable for both physical objects and paper and electronic items and computer files, and also emotional interactions.

In addition to being highly motivated, you must also develop your **persistence.** That is, it is not enough to be highly motivated. You must decide on a direction and focus and then stick to the task no matter what obstacles should arise, and never give up. Use your creativity to develop alternatives to things that have not worked out. Obtain additional knowledge if needed to research the issue.

Here are some quotations to help you think about *the importance of being persistent.*

"Being defeated is only a temporary condition; giving up is what makes it permanent." – Marilyn vos Savant

"Keep on going, and the chances are that you will stumble on something, perhaps when you are least expecting it. I never heard of anyone ever stumbling on something sitting down." – Charles F. Kettering

"Many of life's failures are people who did not realize how close they were to success when they gave up." -- *Thomas Edison*

"Most of the important things in the world have been accomplished by people who have kept on trying when there seemed to be no hope at all." -- *Dale Carnegie*

"Never, never, never, never give up." -- *Winston Churchill*

"One has to remember that every failure can be a stepping stone to something better." – Col. Harland Sanders

"Our greatest glory is not in never failing, but in rising up every time we fail." – Ralph Waldo Emerson

"Patience and perseverance have a magical effect before which difficulties disappear and obstacles vanish." – John Quincy Adams

159

"Perseverance is a great element of success. If you knock long enough and loud enough at the gate, you are sure to wake up somebody." – Henry Wadsworth Longfellow

"Perseverance is failing 19 times and succeeding the 20th."   – Julie Andrews

"The majority of men meet with failure because of their lack of persistence in creating new plans to take the place of those which fail."   – Napoleon Hill

160

"The person interested in success has to learn to view failure as a healthy, inevitable part of the process of getting to the top."
-- Dr. Joyce Brothers

"We can do anything we want as long as we stick to it long enough." *-- Helen Keller*

"You've got to say, I think that if I keep working at this and want it badly enough I can have it. It's called perseverance." – *Lee Iacocca*

****

161

3.7 BACK TO YOUR CAREER ROADMAP

Remember that your ***CareerRoadmap*** should be reviewed and updated monthly. *Try to learn something new every month that adds to your knowledge and value in the career marketplace.* At first this might seem difficult, but as you set in motion a well-orchestrated array of career development activities, you will see progress every single month.

The ***CareerRoadmap*** that was first introduced in *Section 1.6* should be your primary vehicle for coordinating the required orchestration of the many career development elements, and the *Roadmap* is shown below. Don't just "try to remember" what is important and what needs to be coordinated, but rather organize things in a concisely documented manner.

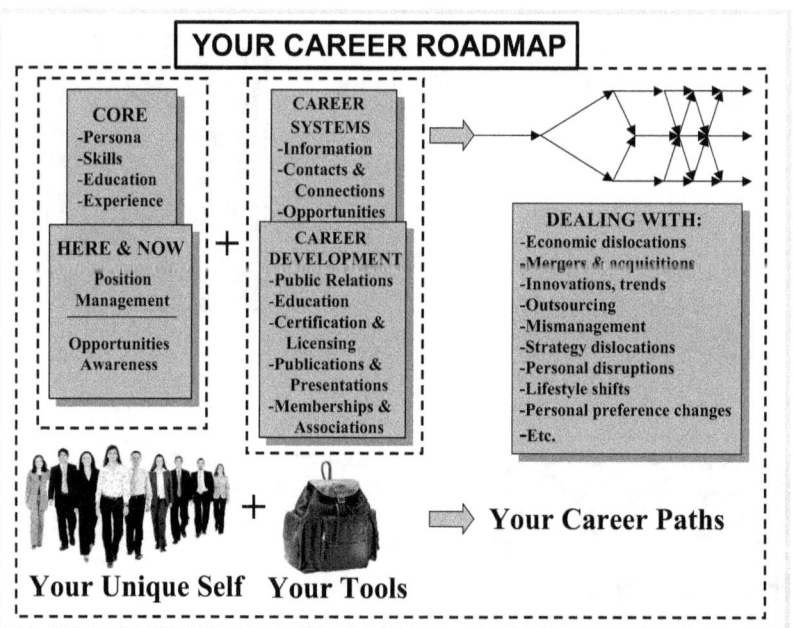

Career goals are imbedded in your Career Roadmap. Goals are NOT to be listed separately without action plans. The reason for this is to totally avoid the common error of making abstract lists of career goals, which are often constantly revised and become a moving target, and also have no linkage to action plans including all of the elements which are needed to be coordinated to meet your goals. Separating goals on a list to stare at as if to impress yourself so that they will happen automatically and magically is a waste of time and a distraction from a real plan. The specific *Career Systems* that have been described numerous times in this book are the concrete support for achieving your career goals. Remember this important truth and proceed accordingly. Without this *high degree of organization*, and without *high motivation* and *high persistence*, you will never achieve control of your career and your goals, but will merely be bounced around by many distracting forces in your life.

You must devote a lot of effort to the maintenance of your *Career Roadmap*, and here are some guidelines in this regard.

- Make sure that anything that is relevant to your career planning which originates from your *Career Information System*, your *Career*  *Contacts System*, and your *Career Opportunities System* is incorporated in your *Roadmap* in a timely manner. Do not let these elements of your career development planning get out of synchronization, but rather make sure that all elements are tightly linked and kept up to date. If you should let things slip temporarily, devote extra time and effort for bringing everything back to complete synchronization.

- At the core of your *CareerRoadmap* is self-improvement, namely education, training, and certification. Do not think that education is something done solely in the past. Many fields change rapidly, and you must keep up to date. Even if you think of yourself as being in a very stable current career position, things can change and you must be prepared. Also, you can bring new perspectives to any position, and your motivation will be renewed by being involved in educational experiences, including socialization with other professionals. With today's rich online environment, there are educational opportunities and choices in every field. Even if you undertake a self-training program either online or via disks or books, keep careful records of this activity, and publicize your completion.

- Also at the core of your *CareerRoadmap* is your inventory of *Accomplishments,* as a result of your *Career Experience*.

When keeping this inventory, do not overlook even seemingly small things. For example, being a member of an important team, even if mostly non-contributory, can add value to your skills. But of course, the more in-depth your accomplishments and the better you document your accomplishments, the more impact on your career profile.

- Often one sees resumes that merely list historical job titles, and then include only cryptic descriptions of job functions. This makes it sound like the person merely showed up and did only routine tasks when they were told what to do. Their value in the career marketplace becomes questionable. Such a resume does not do justice to any real accomplishments or problem-solving or future potential. You never want to characterize a career position in this manner.

- The core of your *CareerRoadmap* must be in balance. Namely, who you are and what you can do must be clear and outstanding, and not raise questions or display confusion. If someone has an excellent educational background but can show few accomplishments, there is a problem. If someone states an impressive list of specialized accomplishments, but no education or training in the particular field, there is also a problem. A highly motivated and persistent individual can dig-in and obtain the knowledge to successfully take on many challenges, but if they lack any formal training or certification, the depth of their accomplishments might be in question. In general, though, documented solid accomplishments trump educational items, as long as any future career opportunity follows closely in line with one's accomplishments. But when fields change, and the future is uncertain, basic education and training, and basic skills, are of increasing importance.

- In the *Roadmap* diagram above, surrounding your core skills are two important items, namely *Position Management* for your current career position, and *Opportunities Awareness and Development*, namely keeping aware of career opportunities, including both internal and external situations. These must be balanced carefully. No matter how discontented you might be in a current career position, you must manage the situation until you have identified and *closed and started* a new career situation. Some people will start a new position on their vacation or a sick leave, in order to be able to return to their current situation if things do not work out as planned or promised. This is not being disloyal but rather judicially cautious. Much has been said earlier about *Position Management* in *Section 2.1*, and deserves review if you are still equivocating about how you manage an existing position but continue to keep aware of both internal and external opportunities.

* *Opportunities Awareness and Development* is of course to be highly structured around your *Career Information System,* your *Career Contacts System,* and your *Career Opportunities System.* It cannot be emphasized enough that a random, occasional, and disorganized effort to look for career opportunities is a waste of time. Chasing down online job postings on an occasional basis, and sending out resumes occasionally when you feel the urge to do so or encounter frustration in your current career situation is equally a waste of time, and will greatly damage efforts to achieve control of your career and your life.

* The *Eight Roadmap Elements* that surround your *Roadmap Core* are to be managed in a coordinated manner. These are not at all independent activities, but are related to one another, and will cause the *Roadmap Core* to evolve in an organized and focused direction. As you become accustomed to an environment of structured career control, you may desire to add your own particular *Roadmap* elements, and this is quite OK, as long as you do not overlook any required fundamentals.

****

3.8 PRIORITIZE AND GET STARTED

Obviously, some things are more important than others, and you don't want to take time away from something more important while you do something else. If you are just starting on building your *CareerRoadmap*, you probably should give first priority to building your *Career Information* and *Career Contacts Systems*.

When building your daily schedule avoid over-booking and overloading. Keep it short and direct initially. Schedule things in priority order and make sure that you finish everything on the list on time. Then you can build out from there. This should help you avoid the common syndrome of making endless lists, then applying tedious prioritization schemes, but being distracted from the important business of getting started immediately. When people list too many things to be done, they often have trouble deciding what to do first, often afraid that if they start on what appears to be important, that they will later find that something else was more important. This causes stagnation, equivocation, and analysis paralysis.

Many of the career development processes and tasks discussed in this book are closely related. You do not want to follow up on any key contacts without being fully prepared, otherwise your effort at communicating with this contact will spoil the opportunity. So career information often precedes any contact identification, but contacts are often found while building career information. Similarly, opportunities are often identified while researching career information.

Once you get started, follow an opportunity as a "trial" through the steps of *Career Information*, *Career Contacts*, *Career Opportunities*, and even *Public Relations* elements. Outline what you would do to follow through – letters, emails, phone calls, etc.

****

3.9 YOU WILL SUCCEED BEYOND YOUR EXPECTATIONS

This ***Prevail, Excel: Career Control Guide*** has provided you with stepping-stones to further your career. There are many things to orchestrate. You can do it. Others have done it. You don't need to be a genius. But you must be very persistent, and constantly build your self-esteem and motivation. Never arrogant, always friendly and supportive. Don't waste time on negative persons. Completely identify and exit negative situations promptly as needed. And finally, the best of all to you in building a very successful career.

****

APPENDIX

ADDITIONAL RESOURCES FOR *"PREVAIL, EXCEL:"*

The information that you can assemble to support your career planning and career actions is voluminous and virtually endless, so you must manage your time and efforts in accessing this information, always focusing on your own career and discarding merely "nice-to-know" stuff. The following, in various categories in alphabetical order, but not necessarily the order of importance, are a number of useful online links which will help your career planning and development.

BUSINESS BROKERS

http://en.wikipedia.org/wiki/Business_brokers
"A business broker is a person or firm who/which acts as an intermediary between sellers and buyers of small businesses. Business brokers, also called business transfer agents, or intermediaries, assist buyers and sellers of privately held small business in the buying and selling process. ..."

http://www.businessesforsale.com/
"Our mission is to connect serious buyers and sellers of businesses and franchises, adding value and making transactions happen. To this end we strive constantly to enhance the site's search function and improve and expand our range of services. ..."

http://www.bizbuysell.com/
"BizBuySell is the Internet's largest and most heavily trafficked business for sale marketplace, with more business for sale listings, more unique users, and more search activity than any other service. BizBuySell currently has an inventory of over 45,000 businesses for sale, and more than 785,000 monthly visits. BizBuySell also has one of the largest databases of sale comparables for recently sold businesses and one of the industry's leading franchise directories. ..."

169

CAREER PLANNING

http://www.careerlab.com/
"We're a career strategy and leadership development firm based in Denver, Colorado USA. Since 1978, 350 brand-name U.S. businesses, non-profits, and educational institutions have hired us to provide Career Strategy, Testing & Assessment, Executive Coaching, Leadership Development, and Outplacement. In addition, every day of every year, we drive remarkable career advancement for upper-level managers and executives, consultants, entrepreneurs, and top professionals—such as physicians [where we have experience with every medical specialty from Anesthesiology to Urology]. This level of experience means we're not beginners. You can trust us. We know what we're doing."

http://www.yourofficecoach.com/
"YourOfficeCoach.com is a web-based coaching and consultation service operated by Your Office Coach®, a training and consulting business owned by Dr. Marie G. McIntyre. Our purpose is to help people resolve the inevitable difficulties and dilemmas that arise on the job."

http://www.jobhuntersbible.com/ and www.dickbollesworkshop.com
"Hi, I'm Dick Bolles. I'm your guide here. This site is designed as a supplement both to my annual, What Color Is Your Parachute: A Practical Manual for Job-Hunters and Career-Changers, *as well as to my new 100 page book,* The Job-Hunters' Survival Guide: How to Find Hope and Rewarding Work, Even When 'There Are No Jobs." *Browse below, and choose a topic that interests you. Or, if you're just looking for vacancies, use our sponsors to the left."*

http://www.quintcareers.com/majors/
"Quintessential Careers is the ultimate career, job, and college site, offering comprehensive free expert career and job-hunting advice (through articles, tools, tips, samples, and tutorials), as well as links to all the best job sites. Special sections for teens, college students, and all other job-seekers (by industry, geography, and job-seeker type) make this site a comprehensive resource for all."

http://advice.careers.org/
"Today, more than 20,000 sites link to Careers.Org and its extensive directory of career resources, college profiles, and regional career directories. Careers.Org is excited to live up to the site motto: If It's About Your Career ... It's Here!!!"

http://www.porot.com/
"With more than 30 years of experience, Daniel Porot is one of Europe's leading pioneers in Career Design and Job Hunting. Daniel and his team of trainers have run workshops, seminars and conferences in 30 different countries throughout the world teaching over 50 different nationalities. To date, more than 70,000 participants have attended their workshops. Daniel co-taught with Richard N. Bolles (author of "What Color Is Your Parachute?") at Richard's annual two-week summer workshop for 20 years. He graduated from INSEAD in 1966 with an MBA, and started his career with Exxon and Amoco, prior to launching his own business in 1971."

http://www.crac.org.uk/
"CRAC: The Career Development Organisation is the independent, charitable organisation dedicated to career development and active, career-related learning. We have a passionate belief that individuals have the ability to achieve their career goals if they are equipped with the skills to do so".

http://careerplanning.about.com/od/selfassessment/tp/assess_books.htm
"Making a well thought out career choice is the most important thing you can do to insure having a successful life at factors you should look at when making a career choice, including your personality, values, interests and skills. The goal of this process, called self assessment, is to find a career that is a good match for you. The books listed here do a wonderful job of helping readers make good career choices."

http://www.careercruising.com/
"Career Cruising offers a suite of online career guidance and planning tools designed for people of all ages. Using our tools, you can find the right career, explore education and training options, build your own portfolio, manage your school's course selection process, or set up a career development network in your community. Learn more about all of these possibilities on our Products page."

http://www.careerplanner.com/
"CareerPlanner.com is a company whose sole mission is to help people find their true purpose in life and to build more fulfilling and rewarding careers. We provide online career testing, as well as free career and "Right Path" information to help individuals discover their true purpose in life and their ideal career. We come at this mission

with a perspective derived from years of hands on management and leadership experience which includes interviewing, hiring, training and coaching a wide variety of individuals. From this vantage point we have gained an ability to see what types of work are right for a person, and what types of work an individual should avoid."

www.Glassdoor.com
"Glassdoor.com is a career and workplace community where anyone can find and anonymously share salary details about specific jobs for specific employers or company and interview reviews describing life on the inside of an employer — all for free. What sets us apart is that all our information comes from the people who know these companies best — either the employees who work there or the candidates who have interviewed there. In the spirit of community, we ask our users to share with each other. That is, before you can access all of the information shared by others in the Glassdoor community, we first ask that you post an anonymous salary, company review or interview review of your own. By working together to offer an inside look at companies, we can open up access and bring greater transparency to information in one of the most important parts of our lives — our work."

http://www.careermag.com/
"Welcome to CareerMag.com, a community providing resources to advance your career. In addition to posting the latest jobs from coast to coast, we offer a variety of career resources to foster professional growth. We even have services designed to increase your exposure to top employers and articles to help you prepare for the next phase of your career."

http://www.careercapitalist.com/
"Lots of buzz going around about a recent Wall Street Journal article suggesting that creating a blog (like this site, but customized to whatever your professional brand is about) is a great way to boost your career prospects. Is that true? Should you create a blog? Can you be the Matt Drudge (pictured at right) of your functional area?..."

CERTIFICATION AND LICENSING

http://en.wikipedia.org/wiki/Professional_certification
This link lists many certifications available, for various professional areas.

http://www.pearsonvue.com/
"Pearson VUE delivers millions of high-stakes tests a year across the globe for clients in the licensure, certification, academic admissions, regulatory, and government testing service markets. It boasts the world's leading test center network, with over 5,000 test centers in 165 countries, 230 of which are fully-owned and -operated Pearson Professional Centers. Pearson Professional Centers utilize a patent-winning design, which was created specifically for high-stakes testing and offers a carefully controlled, consistent testing environment."

http://www.prometric.com/default.htm
"Prometric delivers more than 9 million exams a year for over 450 clients. No other testing firm even comes close. With over 40 years of experience and most industry "firsts" under our belt – there is no provider more qualified. "

CONVENTIONS

http://www.tsnn.com/desktop.asp
"TSNN has available a list of U.S. and global trade shows, consumer events and conferences, which includes updated and newly-added tradeshows delivered on a monthly basis at no extra cost. The lists will be emailed to you in an Excel® spreadsheet and will include most of the following information: …. "

http://www.biztradeshows.com/
"The largest directory of trade fairs, business exhibitions & trade shows, featuring 14000+ live trade events and 4100+ Organizers worldwide."

http://studentcenter.ja.org/Careers/Pages/default.aspx
"Welcome to the JA Career Center. Here you will find information and resources on different job industries, specific careers, and even individual occupations that may be of interest to you. This is the perfect time to explore your skills, interests, and values so you will be able to discover the school subjects and occupations you most enjoy. With this knowledge in hand, you can better prepare for success in your work and in life."

ECONOMIC AND EMPLOYMENT STATISTICS

http://www.bls.gov/
"The Bureau of Labor Statistics of the U.S. Department of Labor is the principal Federal agency responsible for measuring labor market activity, working conditions, and price changes in the economy. Its mission is to collect, analyze, and disseminate essential economic information to support public and private decision-making. As an independent statistical agency, BLS serves its diverse user communities by providing products and services that are objective, timely, accurate, and relevant."

EDUCATION AND TRAINING

http://www.educationconnection.com
Online education and student aid information

http://www.elearners.com/
"Partnering with accredited colleges & universities offering online education since 1999"

http://www.iil.com/
"A global leader in Project, Program and Portfolio Management, Microsoft® Project and Project Server, Business Analysis, Lean Six Sigma, PRINCE2®, ITIL® and Leadership and Interpersonal Skills, IIL [International Institute for Learning] offers innovative learning solutions, training and consulting for corporations and individuals."

FRANCHISES

http://en.wikipedia.org/wiki/Franchising
"Franchising is the practice of using another firm's successful business model. The word 'franchise' is of anglo-French derivation - from franc- meaning free, and is used both as a noun and as a (transitive) verb.[1] For the franchisor, the franchise is an alternative to building 'chain stores' to distribute goods and avoid investment and liability over a chain. The franchisor's success is the success of the franchisees. The franchisee is said to have a greater incentive than a direct employee because he or she has a direct stake in the business. ..."

174

http://www.entrepreneur.com/topglobal/index.html
"While Entrepreneur's *Franchise 500® focuses on U.S.-based franchises, the appeal of franchising goes well beyond our borders. If you've been thinking about buying a franchise--in the U.S. or any other country--consider this list of the top ranking 200 Franchise 500 companies that are seeking international franchisees. ..."*

INTERNATIONAL CAREERS

http://icsc.un.org/joblinks.asp
This site lists 40 links to organizations that are associated with the UN

http://icsc.un.org/
"The International Civil Service Commission (ICSC) is an independent expert body established by the United Nations General Assembly. Its mandate is to regulate and coordinate the conditions of service of staff in the United Nations common system (see below), while promoting and maintaining high standards in the international civil service."

http://www.usaid.gov/careers/
"USAID is an independent federal government agency that receives overall foreign policy guidance from the Secretary of State. Our Work supports long-term and equitable economic growth and advances U.S. foreign policy objectives by supporting: economic growth, agriculture and trade; global health; and, democracy, conflict prevention and humanitarian assistance."

JOB SEARCH

http://nelp.org/
National Employment Law Project, 75 Maiden Lane, Suite 601, New York, New York 10038, phone (212) 285-3025

http://jobsearch.about.com/od/workathomehelp/a/homescam2.htm
http://jobsearch.about.com/od/jobsearchscams/qt/howtotellscam.htm
http://family.auburn.edu/profiles/blogs/warning-avoid-the-dangers-of
Job scams to avoid

http://www.job-hunt.org/
"The purpose of the Job-Hunt.Org Web site is to provide the most comprehensive listing of employer recruiting page links, the best Internet-accessible legitimate job-search resources and services on the Web, and the best and most up-to-date advice from genuine job search and career experts. From the beginning in 1998, the focus is on avoiding scams and protecting job seeker privacy"

ONLINE PRESENCE AND SOCIAL NETWORKING

http://www.linkedin.com/
"Over 100 million professionals use LinkedIn to exchange information, ideas and opportunities"

http://www.awakenyourcareerpreneur.com/2011/07/linkedin-headline-improve-your-profile-by-writing-a-great-headline/
"If you've spent anytime looking at profiles on LinkedIn, you will notice a trend amongst those who share their value and brand in a clear, concise and impactful way. They've spent some time crafting their headline. ..."

http://www.facebook.com
"Facebook is a social utility that connects people with friends and others ..."

http://www.careerbuilder.com/Article/CB-533-Job-Search-Warning-Social-Networking-Can-Be-Hazardous-to-Your-Job-Search/
Social networking dangers

PAY

http://www.payscale.com/
"PayScale is a market leader in global online compensation data. With the world's largest database of individual employee compensation profiles, PayScale provides an immediate and precise snapshot of the job market. Our patent-pending real-time profiling system indexes custom employee attributes (such as industry-specific certifications) and specific job titles for every industry."

http://wiki.answers.com/Q/What_are_the_highest_paying_jobs

PERSONA

http://www.personalitypage.com/
"A website about Psychological Type, based primarily upon the works of Carl G. Jung, pioneer psychologist, and of Isabel Briggs Myers, creator of the Myers-Briggs Type Indicator"

PERSONAL PUBLIC RELATIONS

http://www.marketingyourpeople.com/business-development/relationships
"If you're in professional services, you know how important it is to market yourself. The people you engage with aren't just buying products, they're looking for the experience of working with you. At Marketing Your People, we've created a site to help you market yourself and other professionals in your firm. Each month we'll showcase a topic and give you current resources, links and tips."

http://www.killerstartups.com/
For you own PR possibilities

PUBLIC SERVICE CAREERS

http://www.publicservicecareers.org/
"PublicServiceCareers.org is your source for professional jobs in the NEW public sector - government, nonprofits, NGO's, consulting, contracting and academia. - and for high quality advice and information about public service careers."

http://www.usajobs.gov/
"USAJOBS is the official job site of the US Federal Government. It's your one-stop source for Federal jobs and employment information."

PUBLIC SPEAKING

http://www.toastmasters.org/
"For nearly a century, Toastmasters International has been helping women and men of every background, education level and economic

standing develop the competency they need to become effective communicators and inspired leaders. ..."

http://en.wikipedia.org/wiki/Public_speaking
"Public speaking is the process of speaking *to a group of people in a structured, deliberate manner intended to inform, influence, or entertain the listeners. It is closely allied to "presenting", although the latter has more of a commercial connotation. ..."*

PUBLICATION RESOURCES

http://assessment.tradepub.com/
"Browse through our extensive list of free Business, Computer, Engineering and Trade magazines, white papers, downloads and podcasts to find the titles that best match your skills; topics include management, marketing, operations, sales, and technology. Simply complete the application form and submit it. All are absolutely free to professionals who qualify."

http://careermags.com/
"Free Magazines in the industry. No hidden or trial offers, and no purchase necessary. Magazines are absolutely free to those who qualify. To get your free subscription, simply click on the link for the magazines you are interested in and fill out the form and submit. You may sign up for as many magazines as you like. Remember to fill out the forms COMPLETELY. Publishers will not accept incomplete forms. Please note, we regard your personal information as confidential and private."

RSS, Alerts, and Information Automation
This is a sample of websites which have an "RSS (Really Simple Syndication) reader" which will keep up with real-time updates from a list of websites which you choose.

www.google.com/reader
"Have trouble keeping up with the sites you visit? Read them in one place with Google Reader, where keeping up with your favorite websites is as easy as checking your email. Stay up to date Google Reader constantly checks your favorite news sites and blogs for new content. Share with your friends. Use Google Reader's built-in public

178

page to easily share interesting items with your friends and family.
Use it anywhere, for free. Google Reader is totally free and works in
most modern browsers, without any software to install. "

http://en.wikipedia.org/wiki/News_aggregator and
http://en.wikipedia.org/wiki/RSS
RSS background information

http://www.disobey.com/amphetadesk/
*"AmphetaDesk is a free, cross platform, open-sourced, syndicated
news aggregator - it obediently sits on your desktop, downloads the
latest news that interests you, and displays them in a quick and easy
to use (and customizable!) webpage."*

http://www.feeddemon.com/
*"FeedDemon is the most popular RSS reader for Windows, with an
easy-to-use interface that makes it a snap to stay informed with the
latest news and information."*

TRADE GROUPS AND PROFESSIONAL ASSOCIATIONS

http://en.wikipedia.org/wiki/List_of_international_professional_associations
International professional associations

VENTURES AND YOUR OWN BUSINESS

http://www.inc.com/
*"Inc.com, the website for Inc. magazine, delivers advice, tools, and
services, to help business owners and CEOs start, run, and grow their
businesses more successfully. You'll find information and advice
covering virtually every business and management task, including
marketing, sales, finding capital, managing people, and much, much
more."*

http://www.entrepreneur.com/
*Entrepreneur Magazine is a useful resource for small business
resources, including startups, franchises, and brokered small
business purchases.*

http://www.score.org/
"SCORE offers free and confidential advice to small businesses: face-to-face counseling, online counseling, online workshops and more."

http://www.sba.gov/
"… The SBA helps Americans start, build and grow businesses. Through an extensive network of field offices and partnerships with public and private organizations, SBA delivers its services to people throughout the United States, Puerto Rico, the U. S. Virgin Islands and Guam."

http://www.flyingsolo.com.au/
"Fresh articles from our team of experts are published each weekday. Read how to get going in startup then find out more about technology, marketing and finance. Plus there's plenty on how to work smarter and live smarter, too! …"

http://www.wickedstart.com/public_home
"The name Wicked Start, while irreverent and fun, is also a play on a slang definition of "wicked," meaning masterful. A "wicked start" is a masterful way of starting a business. At Wicked Start, we believe entrepreneurs and small business owners are on the forefront of business today, leading change and innovation with great ideas. Starting a business is one of the biggest decisions that you will ever make, and it can be as daunting as it is exciting. To be successful, you must take lots of personal, financial and planning considerations into account. At Wicked Start, our objective is to combine a practical, manageable business approach with a dose of "heart" to manage these considerations during the entire start-up process. This "heart" is compassion, which plays an instrumental role in how you create, drive and build a successful business on based on principles, integrity, and best practices. By injecting compassion into your solutions, you will find a healthier business in the long term and a healthier bottom line. "

WRITING AND PUBLICATION

http://superperformance.com/10grammaroffenses.php
"The top 10 grammatical and spelling offenses on the web and in the office."

http://career-advice.monster.com/in-the-office/workplace-issues/improve-your-writing-skills/article.aspx
"As more business communications are conducted through email, instant messaging, PowerPoint presentations and other written forms, writing ability can help today's professionals set themselves apart. The ability to write clearly in reports or white papers is necessary to advance."

http://owl.english.purdue.edu/
"Welcome to the Purdue OWL [online writing lab]. We offer over 200 free resources including:
Writing and Teaching Writing, Research, Grammar and Mechanics, Style Guides, ESL (English as a Second Language), Job Search and Professional Writing "

http://www.dailywritingtips.com/
"Whether you are an attorney, manager or student, writing skills are essential to your success. The rise of the information age – with the proliferation of e-mails, blogs and social networks – makes the ability to write clear, correct English more important than ever."

****

INDEX

Page

****